MEET YOUR

Self

The best investment ever.

*You are the one you been waiting for– to seek
and find your highest path ..*

LENA PREMLEENA WETTERGRAN

Paperback: 978-1-967820-27-6
eBook: 978-1-967820-28-3
Library of Congress Control Number: 2025908391

This is a work of nonfiction.

Ordering Information:

Prime Seven Media
518 Landmann St.
Tomah City, WI 54660

Printed in the United States of America

*T*hank you to all of you who supported me so that this book could happen.

To all of you who dared to look inside sharing the wisdom and love that live within us all.

My beloved mother who with her absence made me find my own inner divinity.

My beloved father who did his best and my brothers, you have been my princes.

Friends I have met on my life path mirroring who I am and who I am not.

The here and now that constantly embrace and guide me.

Osho, my master who beyond words reflects my true self and divinity.

Byron Katie for her clarity, love and "watertight" technique "The Work".

Eckhart Tolle for his unique energy and clarity about the wisdom and power of the present.

To all of you who will walk the path and to all of you who have walked the path before me.

With this book I wish to support you as a reader: To find the passion within you and live it. Know that you are born perfect and unique. You are cared for and loved in every detail. Learn to live open and in the present. Here and now is everything. With this book I wish to support you to start exploring your inner world, and to start sorting it out. Mind, heart and being. To let your inner wisdom and natural loving nature come to life. It is not how your life began that is the point but how you choose to live it now. Consciousness is all there is.

FOREWORD

By Roger Nilsson

*L*ena Premleena Wettergran's journey through life has been of importance, joy and benefit to many people as she has generously shared her vast experience, wisdom and knowledge in creating and guiding people since early -90. She also does so generously in this book in a vulnerable and poignant way.

I first met Lena in the early 90s when our paths crossed around a leadership workshop she was co-leading. That meeting led to a lasting friendship. Over the years I have followed Lena on her path as a successful creator and leader of a large number of therapeutic group processes at various personal development training center. Now more commonly under the name "Blissful living". Her creative ability, her enormous, never-ending enthusiasm and her loving wisdom to lead people to a better life have made a deep impression on me. A dedication and love for her calling that few can match.

This book contains a lot of, for me, new knowledge about her life, from childhood until today. A book that gives insights into how to work with clients, which I think psychotherapists of all kinds can learn something from.

The deep spiritual experience that existence offered her at the age of 28 has clearly laid a foundation, a platform on which she has been able to stand firmly through the storms and difficulties of life. This particular experience, a particularly emotional part of the book, is well described as a small miracle. A miracle that was born out of meditation, therapeutic methods, breathing exercises, body psychotherapy and the meeting with an Indian master.

I am convinced that Lena/Premleena is "redeeming" and releasing thousand of people, specially here in Sweden, from their destructive, unaware painful, obsessive thoughts, feelings and behaviors. In order to do so, we must first have helped ourselves, become aware of and "redeemed" ourselves from our "backpacks". To face and learn to love ourselves, so that you can love and understand others.

Perhaps we all have to go through the "dark night of the soul", before it is broken and we can see with clear eyes. To go from painful unawareness to realization and acceptance before any change occurs. As someone said, "Pain is not in the way, it is the way!»

I think Lena's / Premleena book is unique. Perhaps the first book written by a Swede that describes some kind of spiritual, existential awakening that is then followed by a practical description of how to go about "washing off the mental, emotional dirt» that we often carefully inherited through an unfavorable environment. An «original sin» that we can actually, to a large extent, learn from and then be able to accept ... then it lets go. To stop trying to control ourselves into a better life.

"Meet your self" contains much that is known in the spiritual traditions of many thousands of years, but she has packaged her message in a way that makes it easier for those of us living in modern times to understand and absorb that wisdom. Western psychology, in my opinion, lacks a deeper dimension, a wisdom that Eastern psychology has had for a few thousand years.

It is difficult to help someone to a freer life without having experienced and walked that path yourself. The journey Lena/Premleena made helps us closely understand the importance of facing ourselves.

To develop space for awareness and to come out of one's own isolations. Learning to understand that everything and we are all part of an infinite whole. Then we can learn to reduce our judgment, become more accepting and loving. Especially important in our time.

Roger Nilsson - Addiction doctor international world sailor & therapist

CONTENTS

INTRODUCTION

*A*ll that you longing for is already within you! Your heart knows and carries all the wealth. Get to know you and start listening, you are the gift to yourself.

When we stop and allow ourselves to just be for a moment, we all experience peace. A peace and simplicity where everything is perfect just as it is. The only thing that disturbs this peace is the confusion of the mind and thoughts that take us away from ourselves in different ways. So why has this happened? That we live in constant struggle with life and ourselves when peace exists only if we stop and become present for a moment.

We were conceived and we were born absolutely perfect. Nothing was missing from us.We are and have always been completely and totally taken care of. The most natural thing we all once had.

Why is it that we have come to believe that we need to seek validation and security outside ourselves? That we have closed off contact with ourselves. As long as we don't stop and investigate, the result is that we just run on without really knowing where we are going or if we are going anywhere.

We all carry a dormant awareness, wisdom and love within us. It is in fact our true nature. Here and now we can begin to open that door, home and into ourselves.

I remember sitting on a park bench as a five-year-old, looking at a fountain. water constantly splashing up from the center and then falling down again. It is a beautiful early summer day. The sun is shining and it sparkles like diamonds in the water jets. I am so amazed at the cycle that seems to be endless. I sit there and wait for my mom who is shopping in the store right next door. I look at the water and at the same time I see people walking by. Everyone is on their way somewhere. I remember how a sense of wonder washes through me. There and then I see the connection between the constant movement of water and the constant movement of life. I see that within every human being lives this source of energy. It was so obvious, pure, simple and beautiful to me there and then. One thing that puzzles me, however, is that the adult people I see seem to have forgotten it. They walk fast and forward leaning, like they were walking a step ahead of themselves. When my mother comes out of the store, I ask her. "Mom, why have grown-up people forgotten who they are? They don't see the beauty that's happening here. Where do they think they're going? Why do they look so serious?" My mom looks at me and shakes her head. "I don't know" she says shortly and sighs lightly. I take her hand as we walk and I continue to talk about how the water of the fountain is endless. I am happy and jumping holding her hand as we walk home. It's like I understand that everything is a whole and we are it. I remember how obvious it felt to me. That we are one and the same as the water. That we all have a fountain of energy within us. A fountain of energy that is not personal, but flows through us. All water is equal and from the same source.

Later when I am between five, six years, the natural connection with the whole began to shut down. It did so for me for various reasons. But the understanding I have gained over the years has led me to believe that this is the case for most of us. The innocent openness that once existed is closing again. That doesn't mean we can't find it again. We can, that's what this book challenges you to do. For me, that turning point and encounter with self happened when I was twenty-eight years old. For twenty-three years or so I lived in a lost illusion of myself. It was painful. When that innocent, simple openness began to disappear, I closed the door on myself and began to focus outside myself and create a survival strategy instead. What had been so simple, beautiful and self-evident closed in on me.

To open that door again after twenty-three years and to release the longing that lived there. To let my inner fountain begin to flow freely and to begin to live this mystery of life as it is meant to be lived. It is the greatest of gifts. But first I needed to both turn off and forget.

I had to go through many pains and separations before I would be "forced" to stop and look at myself again. It took many years, but when the turn came, it was so natural, obvious and longed for.

We can now choose to stop and put our lives in order. Find the life vision and energy that lives within us. We are not going anywhere and everything we need is here. All the searching and chasing outside ourselves only creates more and more stress. With this book, I wish to give you the gift of finding that you are the friend and the opportunity. That you carry all that you need. You are perfect, your life here and now is perfect.

It is your heart that has the wisdom and knowledge. Not your intellect, where there is only a myriad of questions but no answers. The intellect cannot see the whole, it only sees the parts and builds the idea of the future on old knowledge. Being able to have a loving relationship with yourself means increasing your understanding of yourself. Seeing the bigger picture. To yourself and to life as a whole.

Unawareness of who we are creates stress and a feeling of being separated from life, like a victim in all circumstances. Whereas awareness puts us in touch with our inner source. We can then make wise, true, choices, living more lovingly in joy and wholeness. If we long to live in some kind of paradise, a longing to live in more harmony, love and creativity. Well, then there is only one place we have control over, our inner self, that is where the opportunity is and the adventure can begin. A journey with a beginning but no end. But as long as we don't understand who we are, it's hard to relax in life or see what steps to take. We have confused who we are with what has happened to us. We have locked up unprocessed events and emotions and built our identity on top of that. That's what I did and that's what most of us do. By doing so, we have lost the natural inner contact with ourselves and with it also separated ourselves from the whole and life itself. This creates imbalance, pain and uncertainty. Life can start one way, and there is nothing we can do about it except accept and reconcile. But if we want to live and end life in a more loving way, we can. If we want to find harmony, peace and love, it is by starting to see, understand and open the door home and into ourselves again. Many years ago I created a transformative three and a half day process called Door Opener. During these days we stopped, turned our gaze home into the presence and energy that lives within us. Started to explore and get to know what was trapped. The emotional memories that needed to get air and come to the surface. What personality we have created from our history. What happens when we begin to understand, witness and get to know who we are. Through that become one with the inner natural energy we are. The one we were not separated from as children. To discover the sense of wholeness and love. That it already lives within us. All that we long for is there if we just start to see what blinds us. All we are looking for are natural qualities that we have locked away. We are all the same, just slightly different stories that we bring with us. Almost all the people I met in different processes over the years came, as I also did, in contact with a truer reality within themselves. Where wisdom, answers and harmony prevail. Giving you the opportunity to become conscious is the greatest gift you can give to yourself. You are perfect. All the answers are within you. You are cared for and not alone. Where you are right now is perfect. Choose to stop right here and now. Here on all the energy and everything you need).

What I write about is based on my own experiences. I have created a wheel of life that allows us to understand and sort out in a simpler way. With this book, I want to give you as a reader a way to meet and get to know yourself on a deeper level. A journey between you and you, you and life. The gift that you can find your own truths and create a truer, more creative and loving life with a living vision of life from within yourself and your inner unique longing. Life is your adventure and mystery to explore. To you who are reading these lines right now, I can only congratulate you, in you lives a longing that guided you to read this so that that longing in your heart can then have more space in your life. You are already home. You can either keep reading and just relax and keep letting your inner self guide you.

Or you can keep reading and enjoy all the insights and joy of being you. Making friends with yourself and living you. A wonderful journey, if you ask me, when love, trust in yourself and life can be present. Stop, examine and find the answers within you. Learn to see, understand, reconcile and find that everything you long for is already within you. If you want and long for a new way of living with yourself, there are all possibilities. The love and the answers are there. Turn your eyes and everything is given to you. You are everything and nothing. The journey is open for you to explore.

I looked inside myself and that was the start of a divine journey with myself, from pain and separation, from myself and life, to a life of loving harmony and intuitive guidance.

I have been given the gift of sharing this knowledge of our inner self with many people through courses and individual meetings. The answers are always the same, "Why has no one said anything about this before. It is so obvious". With "New Life Vision" I want to give you the opportunity to realize your life, let your inner self expand beyond what you thought was possible. You just need to stop and open yourself to it.

Being abandoned and rejected by my mother as a child created a great pain and wound within me. With a feeling of not being worthy of love. Not being wanted or belonging anywhere. I was not part of her life. Everything was unclear, disconnection and feelings of exclusion meant that I constantly lived in pain and with a swallowed grief.

The turning point, the transformation and awakening, came when I stopped and turned my gaze home and into myself. An inner journey and process. Sorting out within myself among emotional memories and thoughts that I had been identified with. It gave me the gift of being able to see and live my life lovingly and in trust of what is, inside and out. My focus shifted from being identified with parts of my story to seeing the whole and the space that embraces all. Through being given the opportunity to sort within, I found that all wisdom, creativity and love already reside within me. I stepped out of the way of myself and the adventure of life had begun with me present.

The invisible wings of life had always carried me but with awakening came the awareness to see and understand that the stillness, creativity and richness of life had constantly embraced me with its presence and wisdom. It was the inner longing that had shown me the way. The mystery of life had opened its doors.

With "New Life Vision" I want to share and give everyone who has an inner longing or a chafe within them an opportunity to find their own path and rest in it. For me, life itself is a journey in meditation. There is no separation between you and life. Between you, your feelings and who you are. Loving presence in balance with who you are, here and now, makes for a wonderful and divine life.

This book is a help for you to understand who you are. A help to look at life from a bigger perspective. With my Wheel of Life, you can connect with yourself and explore your own truths. To find trust in yourself and in life. To be able to clean up within you what is no longer helpful to you, sort out to find a way to live in harmony with yourself and life based on your own truths. To be able to see the bigger picture of who you are. Understanding your history and what it does to you here and now. Being able to understand your different roles and who you are beyond them. To dare to listen to your inner longing, your dreams and be able to affirm them. To be able to live in more trust, peace and love.

The first step is to stop and look inside yourself. It is there that you will find the source of your life energy, your truths, and it is there that you can sort out what stands in the way of a full life.

We all have the power within us. But we bind it by holding on to old patterns, thoughts and emotional memories. This is because we have no other consciousness of who we are.

There were many misconceptions that I was carrying. We carry many misconceptions unnecessarily.

Throughout my childhood, at home, at school or elsewhere, no one had pointed out our human nature and how we can live our lives.

So my awakening was a revolution and transformation, from the inside out. Osho, an Indian mystic, came into my life and the mystery of life opened up and melted my whole being. Now, after years of living, sharing and working from wholeness, presence and inner wisdom, it is time for me to write down and share my journey.

One of the biggest misconceptions is that we think we are missing something. That we are not perfect as we are. That what we need should come from outside: love, understanding, affirmation and so on. That we will be whole if we just get it from someone else. The truth is that we are already whole. That we don't need to get anything from anyone. But that we feel good to start living the energy we already are. The fountain I saw as a five-year-old, we all have within us. Like a flower seed that carries its full potential within it, it is also with us. But most of the time, we have not been given any confidence in it. Instead, we have been given thoughts that we should not believe that we are anything. We have shut down in the belief that we would be so much better if we were like someone else. The truest and most natural thing is to find happiness by stopping, sorting out our misconceptions, stepping out of the way of ourselves and starting to affirm what already lives within us.

Creativity is our inner vibrant source of energy. It lives within every human being. This creativity has its unique expression through each of us. Some become artists. Some become scientists. Some work in music. Some work in a shop. Others clean to keep things nice and clean. All expressions are valuable. The misconception is that we think we should be someone other than who we are. Let us be what we are. Nothing else. This life energy or our inner potential has been encapsulated with limiting thoughts.

Just like I once did, most of us live with full focus outside ourselves. Hoping and believing that everything we need will come from someone else. We go from being children, where we may not have felt seen or loved as we would have wished. To becoming an adult, without examining or understanding what our history has done to us. We may hope that our partner will be able to fill the emotional gaps. That's exactly what I did. We hope for someone else to see us. We long for someone to love us.

We want approval and praise. We think and live as if life is not on our side and is instead our enemy. As if what life wants is not the same as what we want. That life does not respond to our desires. That is certainly not true. It is we ourselves who do not examine, become aware and live the life we desire and long for. It is possible to find who we are beyond history.

We think we live separate from the whole. Which we don't, but we think we are.

As long as we don't stop and investigate, everything stays the same. But when we start investigating, life starts to look different.

When we walk in the belief that it will come from outside, we live in separation with ourselves. This creates pain and frustration or just a sense of disconnection.

When we turn our gaze home and into ourselves, we increase our understanding. Then we start to live in contact with ourselves and that makes us live with ourselves and we also live in contact with life. There is no separation. Your inner life, life itself and the whole universe are one and the same.

You already have and are everything you are looking for. You yourself are the friend you have been waiting for.

I had lived in isolation, had encapsulated my entire history and did not like myself. Unconsciously, I hoped that someone would come and love me. Someone would come and redeem me. Someone would come and see me.

Like most of us, I believed that happiness, love and success lay outside myself. That is not true. It was and is in my hands. Everything was and is already here, within me. I just hadn't been given the tools to understand, open up and sort out what was what.

We all know how nice it is when we clean out our closets, drawers and cabinets. How nice it is when we take the car for cleaning and service. When the dentist has done his job. When we throw away what we no longer need. We also need to do this with our inner self. Look from the outside in. Become aware of what is strengthening, what we are thinking, what feelings are stirring. There is only one person who can do that job and that person is you.

Stop, look inside yourself. Clear your mind, examine who you are and find what is true for you... Truth is not a morality, nor a religion. In the present moment lives an intuitive wisdom. It lives in your heart and I call it "your truth". A truth is that a rose is a rose, dogs bark, cats meow and your inner voice tells you what feels true and right to you. This truth has nothing to do with any religion. Your inner self and your inner wisdom is true for you when you understand, no one can take that away from you.

To live a conscious life is to take one's life into one's own hands and to be in a constant living and to some extent questioning of what is our truth. A loving questioning that makes us peel off the veils that obscure our presence in order to see clearly. The Wheel of Life, which I created, is a tool to be able to see and understand one's life in a simpler and clearer way. So we can be in a living process with ourselves and life. A journey that has a beginning but no end. The art of living in harmony with ourselves and life. Allow your life to become whole, to be one. No more separations between you and you, you and life, you and the divine, you and your partner, friends or children.

Life, love, truth, you and divinity are all one and the same. Only old ideas, thoughts and beliefs can blind you from who you are. Find the love within you and what is true for you. Give the awareness within you room to expand. I wish you could understand that everything you seek is already within you. You are not to become someone else, you are already perfect. Get closer and closer to that truth within yourself).

MY LIFE JOURNEY –
LIFE WANTS ME HERE!

*A*ll children are born perfect. Open, trusting, loving and unique. We accumulate experiences in our subconscious. We are like an iceberg where only our surface is visible. It is not the surface, or the top of the iceberg that governs our lives. It is our subconscious and what is below the surface that governs. Getting to know what drives us is the only way to true change and transformation. The way is to stop, go inside and start knowing yourself from within. Examining and understanding goes through the emotions. Then we can accept and see the whole picture. Beyond the story. When I did that, my whole life changed. Becoming one with myself and life. I experienced the love within me. Here comes what was my foundation

Love is never the problem. We are pure love energy. For me to understand that, I need to see the thoughts, feelings and experiences I had accumulated from my entire childhood. Like a wall that blinded me. We have all been loved in different ways. Otherwise we would not be here. When I write about my story, it is from my experiences and insights. From the outside, it looked completely different. I know that people around me have often told me how good I had it. How wonderful my parents were. How spoiled I was. What they didn't see was what it was like for me. Which we rarely do. We interpret and judge what we see from the outside, the surface. What I have written about here, is how I have experienced it from within myself, from as true a perspective as possible. I know I was loved in many ways but the pain that came with the years obscured me. I know that my mom and dad have done their utmost based on what they carried. I love them and my brothers dearly. My mom with her childhood of being in an orphanage for the first years of her life and then being adopted. A secret I found out when I was thirty-five. My father for his upbringing in a religiously free part of Sweden, three younger sisters and a mother who died a little after he left home as a young man. None of them had received much help or understanding about their feelings or who they were or what they wanted with their lives. Few have received that help. With New Life Vision, I hope to give our stories understanding and love so that we can live our lives free to be who we are.

MY CHILDHOOD - FROM BIRTH TO TWENTY-ONE

"*M*aybe, maybe we want you". That's the feeling I grew up with. At the beginning of my life, I was loved and a little princess who would get everything. I was kissed, hugged and cuddled with in moments. Other times, I was abandoned and almost forgotten. One side of me felt like the little cutie everyone wanted and gave the family new love and hope, the other part felt like I had no place at all. Later, both of my parents chose to give me up. First my mother and then also my father. It has reflected and permeated my life in so many different ways. But it has also been the gift for me to deeply examine who I really am.

My first week on earth started with me screaming like all newborn babies do. So that I would not disturb the family and their night's sleep, they put me in the kitchen, away from the bedrooms, so that my cries could not be heard so well. This was advice from the midwife. It was like that in those days. After the third night, I was silent. I can only imagine how those three nights felt inside me. Nobody came. After that I was a quiet and "good" child. I never caused any trouble. I was never annoying.

I grew up as a sled child with two older brothers. My mother was thirty-seven, my father was forty-seven, my brothers were thirteen and eleven when I came to earth. A family created over thirteen years. A family created after a world war that shook an entire world.

Into this family I was born. I felt loved, especially by my mother, like a princess who came straight into the family, but I didn't feel wanted. I was like I never became part of the family. Maybe they didn't want me, maybe I wasn't planned. Don't know the answer to that. Both mom and dad were two very socially active people. They were liked and loved by many. They were away a lot and often had parties at home. They were vibrant and beautiful, but children in those days were not a priority. Not in our family. Not me anyway, sloppy child that I was.

When I was three years old, my mother was at hospital for operation, for a gallstone attack. I was then left with a family I had never met before. There I got to be with completely new people. The family had a son who was around nine years old. A son who was aggressive and "difficult". I remember sitting curled up in a window frame, my whole body shaking with fear and vulnerability. Alone and completely abandoned without knowing or understanding. I look out the window to see if my father is coming to get me. He did, but only after a week or so. A week for a three-year-old is like an eternity. When I got home, I realized that my brothers, who had been at home, were privy to everything that had happened. I was the only one who didn't know, the only one who wasn't included, the only one who didn't understand that mom was in hospital. After that, I had a hard time finding the trust that had previously been so obvious.

When I was five or six, my mother started working. Something she had longed for as she had been a housewife all these years. She hadn't worked since my eldest brother was born, he was now eighteen. It was as if she had longed to get away and out of the family. As I understood it, away from me, as I was the only one left at home. Although my mother slowly started to disappear from me, she was the one I trusted the most. The one I had contact with. When she was with me, she was physical and kissed me a thousand times. She said evening prayers and I felt a strong connection. Something I didn't do with my father in the same way. I felt seen by her. She could look at me and ask how I wanted it. Or how I felt about someone in the adult circle of friends wanting to hug me. "Do you want that? Is that ok?" My answer with a simple wave, yes or no, she respected. So on one level I felt really seen by her. Once when we were going for a drive and I was sitting in the back seat with a small basket bag in my lap and mom as usual sitting with a cigarette in her mouth, she suddenly turns around, looks at me and says wonderingly "I wonder if you will always be this loving?". After a while she stops the car, turns around again and says "yes, I think you will be". At that moment I was the center of the universe. I didn't say anything but I have always remembered that moment.

At that time I neither ate nor talked much. Which was of some concern to my parents. But after a visit to a psychologist with my mother, during which I didn't say a word, they dropped the whole project about me. For better or worse. I was left as I was. Today I can see how that was the best thing for me. They weren't there or understood me, but they also didn't give me clear ideas that I needed to change. They just let me be.

But mom "disappeared" to work. It certainly felt like it. Her energy was no longer at home. I remember going to the bus stop hoping to meet her. But she rarely came at the time she said. Or even on the bus. It was like my longing for her was constantly chasing her even further away. An emptiness and a loneliness filled my life. I looked at my mother as the most amazing, beautiful and wonderful person. Many people loved her, and I was often told how great she was, and how great my dad was. When I was five or six, my eldest brother graduated from high school and moved away from home, and my other brother went to sea for a year. I remember how the apartment we live in becomes like a big empty shell. That the home that had previously been full of life and bustle was now big, empty and quiet. For a few years I had an extra home to go to, the Palmes family with "Aunt Bojan" who lovingly picked me up after kindergarten.

I started school and my life was filled with a friend, something I had not had before. She lived nearby and her mom was home when we came from school. We went there. There was a home and security. I could eat there, something I had struggled with for many years. I had to take an edition that would make me hungry. I weighed eighteen kilos when I started school. Dad had been to the school canteen and talked to the people who worked there, they were not allowed to force me to eat, which I appreciated very much. I didn't talk much either. I was mostly quiet, which I liked. Neither the fact that I ate little nor that I was shy and quiet was a problem for me. It was mostly other people's problems. I really liked my new friend who was an only child and lived with her mom and dad in a rather small apartment. We had a big one-story apartment. They had a second floor, but that's where we were mostly, there was a mom. We became deep good friends.

The years passed and it is mostly the summers I remember. The summer I was born, my mom and dad rented their first summer house, in the Stockholm archipelago. The following year they bought a small house a little further away. Grandpa had died and mom had inherited some money. All summers after that we were in this wonderful little summer house. I think it was my salvation. I loved the summers on the island. There was a wonderful sense of simplicity, freedom, nature and beauty.

Out there I had my first real summer job at the island bakery, that's where I was confirmed, that's where I met my first boyfriend. In those days, people moved out to the country. You never went into town. Mom and dad might have gone to Skåne or visited friends, but I was there from the time school ended until it started again.

As a child I was often sick. I had throat infections, colds, vocal cord infections, etc. One day when I was eleven years old, I was home from school because I had a new infection in my body, which neither of my parents liked. I didn't understand why they were so hard on me for it. I just wasn't supposed to be sick. They weren't the kind of people who used to be sick. My dad used to boast that he had never had a sick day or been home from work in his life.

On this occasion, which was to influence my whole life, I went downstairs and lay down on the sofa in the living room for a change of pace. Then I hear my mother coming down the stairs. She is wearing a beautiful outfit, with high heels and a handbag on her arm. I think she is so beautiful. When she comes down, she sits down next to me in an armchair. She starts talking "Lena, I'm not going to stay here anymore, I'm going to leave now". I have now almost completely stopped breathing and say nothing. She continues "I will never be able to be the mom you want who bakes buns and stays at home". I start crying. I cry hysterically. But she is heading for the front door. She says something about maybe she'll be able to pick me up later on, but she doesn't know anything about it right now. She says that when I turn twelve, the law is such that I can choose for myself. I already know what I want to choose. I want to go straight away, I want to go now, which of course I can't. There is a man down the street waiting for her. She leaves with me crying, saying that "everything will be fine". I don't remember anything else from that day and was probably in shock as I had not realized that this would happen. I remember that as a five-year-old I had a dream that my mother would move and asked her then if it was true. But her answer had been that she would never do that. I had believed her and remember how I then happily crawled up on a chair and confidently helped her with the dishes.

My mother's move and my parents' divorce was a big shocking turning point for me. Did not understand. Was it me that was at fault, no other parent had divorced. It is not something 'you' do. At the same time I got glasses and braces. My best friend had also disappeared when she became ill and then moved away. I was not told what had happened there either. I had to grow up fast now. Nothing was safe. It became my father and me. A father who was well-liked in social contexts but completely unaware of what a little girl needed. I became his helping hand with a focus on his well-being. My mother, who was adopted, had been in an orphanage until she was three years old and then had a family to come to with a loving father and a cold mother. She herself was never a wanted child. This is something I learned much later. My father was the oldest of four siblings where he was the only boy. His mother died when he was a teenager. Feelings he had bottled up deep inside. My role was now to keep him happy. My needs were not important, his were. It's on him my whole life depends when mom disappears.

At the same time as my mother moved away, my childhood friend also disappeared. She had had strange symptoms at school and I had tried to help her. She was ill and disappeared into hospital. Her mother, whom I liked very much and she liked me, did not tell me what had happened. I didn't understand, everything that had happened was so confusing. Her mom and dad may have become friends with my parents. So they certainly had an awareness of what had happened. When my friend came out of the hospital, they moved away to another part of Stockholm. We kept in touch but it was difficult. I, in my situation, would have had to grow up and become big in one day. She had gotten sick and was much more vulnerable and became more like a child again.

My father had many great talents and was very musical. He wanted us children to be able to play an instrument. He hadn't succeeded with my brothers so he hoped for me. I played the piano with mixed feelings as I think everyone does at first. The strange thing was that when things started to go well for me and I would play at some shows, he never came. That made me start riding on the sly instead. The piano lessons started to smell like horse. He sold the piano in a flash without warning.

We never talked about what happened. Seven years in piano school and then horses and horse jumping.

I became quite good there too, but without outside support it was difficult for me to continue.

I gave that up too. Skiing, which had always been a great interest of my father's, we were able to share and we went to the Alps together a few times. It was happiness and something I continued for many years.

My mother is slowly disappearing further and further away from my life. One day I am asked if that is my mother on the front page of the newspaper, at the bottom of a small notice that a marriage has taken place between a man who works in the World Bank and is an advisor to governments. It says her name is something completely different now. The pain inside me, the alienation, I cannot put into words. Not even being told what is happening. I feel so insignificant. Luckily I have my dad, he needs me. Every time I hope and believe that my mom and I will get closer, she disappears further and further away. Her new husband has important jobs and they move. First to Skåne in southern Sweden, then to Africa and finally to Asia and Jakarta. Our meetings are short and sporadic. They always end in great pain, betrayal and pent-up grief on my part.

One of the times I come to Skåne. I'm thirteen years old, I'm going to spend Midsummer with my mother and her husband, my stepfather, and I'm filled with happiness. Finally we will meet, mom and I. My mom picks me up at Hässleholm Central Station. We get home and I remember how I happily roll on the big lawn in front of the house. After a while we have had dinner and we sit in the greened summer evening. "Well", says mom "Tomorrow Gunnar and I are going away, but you don't have to worry, you'll get to celebrate midsummer with wonderful friends on a farm in Ängelholm". I feel like my heart is going to burst and break. It takes a while before I run up to the room I've been given as mine, in this big house they live in, crying. Mom comes and sits quietly with me. But no meeting takes place. Then I stay for two weeks on the farm I have been sent to. I don't want to go back to my mom. My insides have broken. Everyone in that family knows my stepfather since many years. They know he has little love or understanding for children. They all feel the grief I carry and do their utmost to take care of me as lovingly as they can. I remember how the father in the family would often make up jokes like putting hairspray under my arms instead of deodorant to make me and all of us laugh. Mom and her husband come for coffee once. No one says anything about what happened. I decide to stay and then go home to my father. The pain inside me is buried under other disappointments. Several meetings take place in the same painful way. I have expectations that are natural for a child in the situations that prevail. One summer I am confirmed and my mother comes to 'visit'. She comes as one of the other guests. I had longed, waited and wanted nothing more than to just be with her. She laughs and socializes. Then, as one of the guests, goes back home after the courtship. I understand nothing. There is never a meeting. She never asks me how I am. Dad puts up with it and I am just 'nice'. No other adult understands or asks how I am. Alone on dark summer evenings. Dad in town. Even then, no one asks how I am. Everything is perfectly fine, normal and beautiful on the outside when my insides are breaking.

One fall, when I started school, she came to meet me. She is home briefly in Sweden without her husband. I am to live with her. During the first night I get a headache and fever. The days pass and I can't move my head. The fever rises. She has so many friends to meet and she doesn't have time for me to be sick, she never has. I can't remember a time when she was there for me when I was sick.

This time, a friend comes to visit my mom after a few days. I have a fever and can't lift my head from the pillow. "Lena must not be very well," says the friend. That afternoon, my father comes to pick me up and takes me to the doctor. Meningitis was my reality. All these events with mom who could never be there for me. I loved her more than anything. As we do as children.

One day on the bus to school, the most horrible of thoughts and feelings come over me. What if she dies? It just can't happen. Fear takes over and I don't understand why. We didn't talk to each other very often as she lived so far on the other side of the world, in a completely different time zone where it was both expensive and difficult to call. Something I felt my father did not want to pay for. Here and now on the bus, my fears came to the surface and it became clear to me how strong the longing for her was and the fear of not being with her, if she were to die. It just could not happen. I quickly shut down these strong feelings and went to school

When I graduate, my dad gives me a trip to Jakarta as a present. My happiness is unimaginable. I travel and leave my father. A father who longs for his freedom to live. I am the only one traveling. My brothers who now have their own families and partners as far as I know were never even asked to go and visit.

The time to come is like paradise for me. To finally be able to be with and get to know my mom. At first it was a strange feeling. My mom, but my mom that I don't know. Inside me I was like a child who constantly longed. Now finally. However, I only got parts of her. Her husband was puzzled and uncomfortable with me being there. This "child" who had now come into their lives. The idea that I could only stay for three months put him at ease. I was not fully welcome. Mom had a hard time dealing with the situation. But for me, the experience of being with her in her life was paradise. Something so natural and obvious to be and get to know with my mom. I also had to come to a country where the warmth, plants, fruits and beauty were tangible. It was in many ways a spiritual country where different religions were a natural part. It was poor, but in every eye there was an inner richness, a harmony and a trust in life. I experienced an outer luxury with my mother and her husband, but the inner peace I experienced was the greatest luxury. All the people I met were so beautiful. On the outside we had a cook, a laundress, a night watchman and a driver, all beautiful, proud and happy. The driver's job was to take my mother and now me wherever we wanted to go. His integrity and dignity were steely. He was proud and he was wise at his young age. He was the one I spent the most time with as traveling in the city often took a lot of time. He told me about reincarnation for the first time. He told me about spirits and how they saw life as never ending. We just changed our bodies, as he put it. He had no idea where Sweden was on the surface of the earth. That alone affected me. A completely different mindset than the one I had. I could not meet him with known thoughts and ideas, but only through the contact we made through our hearts. It took me to a quiet wondering about who we are as people here on earth. It was great, amazing and incredibly valuable to me. It was also an incredibly beautiful country with temples and women beautifully adorned dancing in a way I had never seen before. That my mother and I went on vacation to Bali. This is 1973/74 when everything was innocent and pure. The nature was divinely beautiful. A lonely vacation with just mom and me. It had never happened. I "drank" every moment. All this gave me very deep impressions.

Back to Jakarta and the lives that mom and her husband lived there with dinners every night and socializing got a boyfriend. A Norwegian boy who lived in Jakarta. His family were ship owners. He was the new generation that would take over. Having my own contact in Jakarta made me feel safe. A contact my stepfather could not control. It gave me more than one reason to be there. He was transferred to their office in Singapore, but it was still better and closer to mom than between Jakarta and Stockholm. I traveled home and quickly back again. Singapore with the boyfriend Mom and Dad liked this Norwegian boy a lot. He wanted to marry me, which they thought was great, especially Dad. All the hassle of taking care of me was then over. My boyfriend was the old type who asked for the girl's hand in marriage first. I knew nothing but started to understand. I wasn't there yet at all. I just wanted to be with my mom. I realized that engagement was near. My father was suddenly coming to Singapore. I couldn't breathe. Talked to mom over the phone " you don't know what love is, honey, marry him". I couldn't. It became clear to me that I was in Singapore to be near mom, not because I was in love. Going to see mom and my stepfather in Jakarta and trying to get them to want me there. It doesn't go so well. Their plans are different. I have no place in their lives, it becomes clear. The months that I do get to stay before I have to leave become extremely important. Mom and I meet in emotions and in important conversations. She cries and so do I. Small meetings beyond words. Her pain and mine meet in helplessness and the situation becomes clear. She is not "free" to love me. Her husband, my stepfather, has the so-called power. As I am going home to Sweden, they are also traveling. We are in Bangkok at the same time. Staying in different hotels. I in one, they in another. We don't even eat dinner together. Mom calls and says they have other plans. I am nineteen years old and out in a world I have only recently begun to know. I'm crying my eyes out in my bathtub in the hotel room.

Anyway, I traveled home with the hope that when my mother and my stepfather, during the next year, would move back to Africa, I will be able to come there. Go to university there and live with them. That was what my mom and I had talked about and we both had that wish... Mom had said she wanted that and she would talk to her husband about it. With that, I'm traveling home happy, even though I didn't get to stay and celebrate Christmas with them. They are going on their own vacation to a paradise island where I was not welcome to join them.

Just before I left for home, my mom tells me about her and her family's good friend. She has been seriously ill for many years and that she will now receive a new type of treatment that will help her. She writes in her letter that she thinks she and mom will live the same amount of time.

My mom and I are happy about this news. She had meant a lot to all of us. In an aside, my mother says that if she were to become ill, she would want it to go to her head because then she would not have to be involved.

I come home and it's a little before Christmas. My father has met a new woman. Overwhelmed by emotions, experiences and confusion in everything that had happened, I had a hard time taking in the new situation. I didn't understand anything at the time, but later I realized that she loved my dad, but she didn't want his children in her life. She had probably thought that I was a closed chapter and would stay with my mother. I came home lost but with hope. A hope that the good life with mom would continue. It was a short-lived hope. Mom comes home soon after with a brain tumor. She arrives at Stockholm airport. She went in blue light in the ambulance to the Hospital. She speaks English and has no idea where she is. She and my stepfather had been on a trip to various islands, including Papua New Guinea. There were no doctors there but my mother's husband had started to see signs that she was ill. They traveled to Sydney, where they were advised to fly home quickly. This was serious and she would be hospitalized there. Having her husband in Jakarta and us children in Sweden was not what they recommended.

Mom's quick return home with rapid surgery was overwhelming. On the day of her surgery, her friend who had died a week earlier was buried. My dad was at that funeral while my stepdad and I sat outside the operating room. Everything was so confusing.

Everything is going well with the operation, i.e. mom survived. My brothers and our stepfather are going in. While I have to wait. Mom had opened her eyes and said I was dead. But after a while, I also get to go in and see this beautiful woman, who was my mother, completely changed by the operation.

The week passes, my stepfather leaves for his important mission in Jakarta. My brothers have their lives. I, who have not yet found a life here in Stockholm, will be the one to visit my mother with one of her good friends. That will be my life for the next few months. She can't speak. She just looks at me like a child. My inner pain varies with an empathy, love and helplessness.

One day comes and I am there with her. Her friend is there too but lets me have my time with mom. I hold her hand and she takes her last breath. I feel peace inside me. Mom had been unreachable for a few days. It's time and just as it should be until nurses come in and take over. The feelings inside wash over me. Everything comes up like an internal volcano. I am told to pull myself together and given strong tablets. My brothers come and we have to say goodbye for now. Everyone then goes home. I remember standing out in the parking lot alone and completely frozen. Where do I go now? Everything was over.

I am now twenty-one years old. A twenty-one-year-old whose longing for her mother has only become clearer and stronger. Now she was gone forever. Now I could not even hope. A father who disappeared into a new life. Two older brothers with their lives who also did not get what they longed for.

I had grown up with a loving mother for the first few years. Then, slowly and step by step, she had disappeared. First through work, then by moving to Skåne, then Africa, then Jakarta and Indonesia, now she was gone forever. A mother I had always wanted and longed for. A mother who carried her pain of not being wanted and loved herself. I grew up with my dad when mom left and my brothers were already grown up and had their lives. I became my father's support. Lived to make him feel good. He found his life anew, where neither I nor my brothers were welcome. He let his new relationship take over. Just as my mother had done. Dad couldn't and didn't have the financial strength to be there when mom died. I pray and cry for him to come, but he can't, he says. The experience of being left alone and having to take care of myself is strong. When mom dies, it's like it closes inside me and I have to give everything to survive. What is life about? Is this all that was? Who am I in all this? With all the pain and confusion that I closed inside me, it was hard to feel the answers.

I think my mom and dad would have really loved each other. But their emotional knowledge was zero. They closed in and closed off. In that, there was only a split and separation that came as a result. That's what we all do when we don't have access or even dare to feel our emotions.

As I turn twenty-one and step into adulthood to begin to see what I will become here on earth, I am more lost, lonely, scared, hurt and sad than ever. Shutting down was my only way out. I who once had access to life and the greater aspect was now completely shut down and angry at what I then called God. Had no other word. If this is the meaning of my life then I want no part of it. It was mom's passing and death that had opened a sea of emotions, they had to go. The hope that she and I would meet again was now gone. I was not 'done' with her and my relationship, now she was gone forever. What did God, life want with this? All my own thoughts, feelings and the meaning of life were in one big chaos.

LIVING CLOSED DOWN.
BETWEEN TWENTY-ONE
AND TWENTY-EIGHT.

*N*ow life has come to a halt, a full stop and I had no one to talk to, as I saw it. I was probably in a state of shock. I was used to dealing with my own. I was shut down and didn't know any better. I remember how when I was younger I often cried myself to sleep and my one brother heard it. He came and lay down in my bed and asked if I did that often. I had answered "yes". He had then asked me never to do it again. That I would ask for help, but I never did. Who would I ask? It was like I had gray cement inside me. If any man expressed that he loved me, I could not receive it. I felt nothing and I felt that I had nothing to give. The years that followed were filled with a sense of just surviving. I drank a lot of alcohol, vomited a lot. I had constant problems with my body. Stomach ulcers, colds with throat infections, severe sinus infections and cell changes in the abdomen. Everything followed one another. I lived in infidelity and lies.

Needed to survive and I earned my money. My father had changed our bigger apartment to a smaller one. I would live in it. Everyone had taken the furniture they wanted with them when they moved. Mom had taken hers when she left, my brothers had taken theirs and now Dad had taken his too. I, who had never left home, never had time. I had to take what was left. It wasn't a big problem because things haven't played an important role in my life. I've always seen myself more as a traveler through life than building security outside myself. But during this period everything was so gray. My father remarried a new woman and disappeared into their new life and home. It was also a shock. I hadn't realized that he had longed for something else too. Now he disappeared into that relationship and I got the apartment with all the furniture that no one else wanted. Everyone had left home before me. First my eldest brother when I was just over six, then my mother when I was eleven, then the next brother when I was around eleven, twelve. And lastly my father now that I was twenty-one. For a normal twenty-one-year-old, a three-room apartment is great. But for me it was horrible. I was not wanted anywhere. Left in this apartment that was a choice of my father. Nobody wanted me, neither did I. Small addictions to drinking when I was away. Mom and dad had always drank at parties. I started doing that too. Mom had always smoked and thought it was great. "Lena," she'd said, "there's nothing as good as cigarettes. They are sensual, you can do it alone, you can do it with others, ask for a light, or ask for a cigarette..." I started smoking. It was like an unconscious bond of love between me and my mom. I ate buns and chocolate. Even this with tears in my throat. There was so much longing for my mother and this, for lack of anything else, became my unconscious comfort.

In the years that followed, I lived as if I did not exist. By that I mean that I only lived as was expected of me. My own needs did not exist. Work took all my energy and made me feel nothing. A beautiful man came into my life. We got married, but as sad as it may sound, I was never in the picture myself. My mother-in-law had a lot of influence over the man I married; I had longed for a family, and now I had it. With big Sunday dinners. What I lacked, he had gained in his family. As an engagement ring we used my mother's old ring, incredibly nice but mine. My dad paid for our entire wedding party. My brother paid for the honeymoon on his sailboat. I had the apartment that was the deposit on the house we later bought. I was the one who, through my family, would pay for me to be loved. It was painful to feel that this was the case. I was already a wounded girl. He had mom, dad and family around him. I had none of that.

My father remarries. His new wife was not interested in us children. She had met Dad when I was away with Mom. I think Dad's desire to live with a woman again was strong after all the years with 'just' me. It was more important than his children. To have a wife twenty years younger at quite an old age. She loved him but not his adult children. The pain in my chest was strong. I tried to live a normal life without showing anyone how I felt. I had no answers of my own. One day my husband starts talking about how he wanted us to have children. He looks at me lovingly and says "Imagine when we have grandchildren!". Children!!! I had never thought that far ahead. I didn't even like playing with dolls as a child. The panic inside me comes to the surface. But since I can't communicate what I feel, I pretend it's nothing. We had a big social gathering where we drank a lot of alcohol. It was my salvation.

I didn't subconsciously want anyone to ever feel the way I had felt. I didn't realize it then. But I felt it. My husband had no idea what I was carrying around. He, who had always been loved, with a more functional family still in his life, had an obvious longing and desire for children. I did not. I was just in shock and terrified. I was an unredeemed little child on the inside. How on earth could I take care of a child? Intuitively I knew I would do something else before then. Just didn't know what?

That's where the clear flight away began. It led to me being unfaithful, a divorce and me entering a new relationship. I was the one who cheated, taking on all the guilt and shame. The feeling that everything was my fault was obvious to me. I left without talking, couldn't, about what had happened or what I felt. I left everything in our home and lived my life out of guilt and then I had to pay off my debt somehow. I showed that by not "taking" anything with me. I was the bad one, the horrible one and went from the ashes into the fire. Straight into the next relationship. Without anything. The man I had been cheating with. He "wanted" me more than anything. I said yes. But in the back of my mind there was a voice saying "Stop". But I didn't listen. Stop for what? I didn't want to feel, I didn't dare.

I moved in with the new man. Many things were fine. But he was over twenty years older than me. He had grown children who didn't want to see me. Good for me as I felt then. The man was a father figure. However, I did not see this.

The pain inside me became stronger and more obvious. My body had started to tell me off as I had had many problems with my body over the years. Nothing I talked to others about, everything I kept to myself. But one morning it just happens. I'm home alone, about to leave for work. The sunlight falls weakly through the window as if to say 'welcome' and I feel I can't hold it in any longer. My arms stretch up in the air and my body falls to my knees, a plea for help comes crying out of me. A prayer for help. Alone, I could no longer handle the inner pain and numbness I was carrying... Totally defeated, I hear the words "I can't and I don't want to live like this anymore", "help me". The body with ulcers, cell changes, severe sinusitis, inflammation of the mammary gland quickly takes me to hospital. Constant nightmares of my mother sitting in a hospital bed looking at me with guilt in her eyes.

Where can I have a "vacation" from this life, where can I find peace? How can I get rid of this heap of pressed pain, like cement inside me? In complete pain, resigned and in tears, I lie on the floor.

Help came in a very natural way. I started getting tips from friends about books I could read without asking. A woman came into my life who gave me a massage, a connective tissue massage. She came to mean a lot to me. She talked about how I needed to breathe, not just when I smoked, which I did. One of my "connections" to my mom. She helped me to change my diet. I, who had always had a hard time eating meat, was now 'allowed' to stop. As a child I had only picked at my food. Meat was difficult for me, but I had to 'tighten up'. Now my awareness of food began to change. Among other things, I would drink a-lot of herbal tea throughout the day. She helped me through my first fast, which I have done several times since. Immensely valuable to the whole system. She became like a loving mother figure to me. All the help that came, I never connected to the prayer I had had, it just felt natural and easy. I guess that's how miracles happen every day in our lives. Natural, quiet and simple. Living suspended and unconscious was equal to pain. When small steps in a different direction began, my life became not so painful anymore. It seemed that when we take a step in a more conscious and loving direction, life gives us even more of the same.

AN AWAKENING. I GET PASSION FOR MY OWN LIFE AND WHAT IS BEYOND HISTORY. TWENTY-EIGHT.

I was not a seeker but became a 'finder'. It has never happened to me before that I have done this as an adult. As a child, having conversations with God and asking for help had once been completely obvious and natural. But that was many years ago, many years completely gone. But now that the inner pain is too tangible and the way I live is not something I want to continue with. Then this complete surrender came back. I don't know where to go. The feeling is that I would rather die than continue like this. The help that came my way was like little drops of love, but more was needed. After falling on the floor crying, I get dressed and go to work as if it was a normal day. One day my brother calls and recommends an unusual doctor out in the south part of Stockholm. I call and make an appointment.

On shaky legs, I come out to him at his clinic a week later. I had no idea what he was going to say or do. He sits down across from me, looks me in the eye and tells me that I don't know who I am. That was nothing new. But he tells me that I am energy and that I am like a four-year-old or a ninety-four-year-old, nothing in between. My tears rise inside me and he sees. "You feel sorry for yourself" he says. I stammer something about having two older brothers who are not there for me, that my mother died. I can't even put into words that my father is not there. Then he tells me bluntly "you are the only one who can take care of yourself and have the task of liking you". "It is only you yourself". Between tears I say something that makes him respond. "Ah, you think you are a victim". Think I'm a victim? I am a victim. That is the truth.

His words coming at me are harsh, the tears I swallow down, but somewhere inside me I know he is right. I was a victim in all that happened.

Another meeting with him a week later. He asks me if I have five thousand kronor and if I have any children. I answer yes to the first and no to the second. "Good, then call this woman and do this process". I get a note in my hands. Crying, shaking with the note in my hands, I went home and called. A month later I would begin a kind of therapeutic journey with the goal of freeing myself. A twelve-week process. What on earth had I signed up for? But as I saw it, there were no other options. This or die.

The doctor had told me to write down and tell about my life. Especially about the time before I became a teenager. My papers looked at me blankly. I had no memories.

A few weeks later, I woke up early one morning with a tremendous pain in my left breast. I had a fever and I felt it rising. My first thought was that I was in the wrong bed. But the pain and fever got stronger and stronger. I rushed to the hospital and doctor with my then boyfriend. I sit there in the waiting room at hospital in Stockholm and wait. The fever rises even more and I become more and more confused and dizzy. The doctor arrives and I have to lie on a bed. "Have you given birth recently?". Children, I who have been terrified of having children when my ex-husband asked me happy when we would have children! How could he ask me that? But in all the examining and all the fever and pain, which was immense and painful, I see myself. The question of children and my mother showing up with her cancer that took her life. Would she not have wanted me either? What luck that I will soon start digging into my history. Suddenly I realized that everything was connected. I was bedridden for a few weeks and during those weeks, my inner journey began to open doors that I would grasp a few weeks later. How perfect was that!

There I am, lying on a mattress in a basement in central Stockholm. The year is 1983 and I am twenty-eight years old. I hold a pillow tightly in my arms. I don't know how long I've been lying here. It does not matter then. I am beyond time and space. There are others around me but I hardly hear them. All presence is here and now with me. My whole body vibrates and my whole being is alive. Do nothing, everything happens by itself. A door has opened inside me. Tears, feelings and images have come to the surface. I see and I understand. Everything that I experienced as a child and that I closed inside me.

I have loving support around me that creates a sense of security. A therapist, a therapeutic process and assistants. The mattress I lie on has embraced me many times by now. My inner journey I started is twelve weeks long. Lying on the mattress and consciously breathing to feel has become a natural part of opening the door to the inner world. Focus and attention are home in myself. A few months have passed and an understanding has emerged about the thoughts and feelings I have been carrying. More and more I stand on my own side and examine what I have experienced and felt. Getting help to question and see. Through this, I can begin to sort out what is mine and what is not. Begin to understand the experiences that have subconsciously guided my life. Here I am now in this process to get the unconscious and what has been suppressed to come to the surface. In this process, meditation and breathing have been very helpful. Breathing helps to find the deeper unconscious layers that I carry. Breathing helps emotional memories that have been stored to come to the surface. At first it is a struggle but with each breath it becomes easier and easier. Breathing and movement open up for the life energy to come alive again. Unlike my experience in the past of being like cement and stuck inside.

On this particular day, I become aware that the body knows, in it lives a wisdom, that the energy within me knows and it is it that takes over. It becomes clear how "I" step out of the way. Everything happens by itself. It is only fear that can hold the energy back. But during these months, the confidence within me has grown and on this particular day everything opens up and no control stands in the way. Total presence comes the more I breathe and let go. I experience how the body and energy take over and let what is to happen happen. There is no need for "I", a liberation and at the same time a sense of wonder. It seems as if the body, the energy, has total trust and knows. An inner picture becomes clear to me, it is like a river that just flows forward. The river, the energy knows which way it is going. Relaxation takes place and gives the experience of letting go into total wonderful wholeness. A feeling beyond all separation, just a divine whole. Floating in the universe. I hear the therapist come up to me and she asks me to slowly finish the exercise. I hear the therapist talking to me, but the experience continues. Her words are completely insignificant. The experience is total, beautiful and liberating. Somewhere there is an awareness that "I" am going back and after repeated attempts on her part, I "tighten up". The experience that I am one with the whole and should now sit up and talk so she understands that everything is ok. It is difficult but slowly I sit up with the others to end the day. I remember how I struggle to appear "normal". Inside me there is such a longing to just lie down again and feel the vibrations of being one with everything and this vibrating energy of love. This infinite universe within me. I cannot resist. As the others slowly go home, I lie down again. The therapist who was extremely loving lets me continue. All of a sudden it is as if my inner self opens up further, there is only love, power, trust and the most beautiful of experiences. This divine presence, so infinite, my whole being is like a vibrating peaceful, living ocean of love. The therapist speaks. "Lena come back, we are going to finish". If only she knew. It's not me who does or decides anymore. I had given up and let all the energy take over. Whatever wants to happen, will happen. There are tears without a story. It's just a great relief, I can't, I don't want to resist. The power is total. The therapist comes and sits next to me for a while when she realises what is happening. "Just keep breathing and have faith". Her soft voice is nice and inside me there is a voice that says that there is no "I" doing anything right now, everything happens by itself. I can not influence. It's like a warm loving mass fills my whole being. Like a volcano of healing energy, I feel filled and empty at the same time. Liberation and warmth are spreading. Everything is like waves of soft energy within me. Tremors occur in the body like electricity. My whole self is alive. The presence of awareness is everything.

My experience is that I vibrate love. An unconditional divine presence. I am one with everything.

The body breathes by itself. Waves of energy come and go, by themselves. I feel that I see everything from the outside. Everything really happens by itself. I am the one who sees and witnesses. Like the "genie in the bottle" experience. I realize that who I am has nothing to do with my history.

What I experience is just wholeness and vibrant energy. I had opened the door to my inner self. The door that had been closed since childhood. Now I could see that nothing was wrong, broken or separated. I feel whole and vibrating with the whole universe. I see and I understand. The realisation is that this is the truth about me, well, then it must be everyone's truth. We are one. I experience divinity without knowing what it is or having any ideas about it. Beyond the idea of any religion. If I am divine, then so is everyone. In my mind, silent questions rise to the surface by themselves but also the answers come up. I experience the whole within me. The therapist asks me to sit up and come back. I struggle to do as she says, but what happens in me is beyond my doing. I see that the body sits up while I just witness. The body breathes by itself and bliss is all I feel. Nothing else. I see myself coming out into the street in the dark night. The body moves with my presence and everything. I don't remember much else from that night but I come home. I could not put the experience into words. Nor does it do it justice. But the experience came to transform my whole life. As a result, there was joy and a total connection with life itself.

A few months earlier I had no idea that this was possible. All the healing, all the insights, all the emotions and all the loving energy. That within us lives the ability to move beyond separation and pain. A few months earlier, I had fallen down on the bedroom floor in a prayer for help. My mind was then in a mess of unconscious thoughts, locked up emotional memories, events, shocks, confusion, pain, longing and a lot of upside down love. I had no idea that all the power, love and possibilities were already inside me. That it was my history, my thoughts and all the emotions I put inside me that determined how I interpreted life and what stood in my way. That I repeated my patterns again and again. I created everything from my history and unconsciousness. I had locked up my feelings. Which had separated me from my inner self. Unconscious thoughts that I was wrong had ruled my life. Trapped emotions layered on top of each other had prevented me from being in touch with my inner truer self. It was painful. It had been like my inner self was solid frozen cement. Now I was lying here and the greatest of gifts had come to me, the gift of understanding who I am, feeling and allowing the energy of life to come to life. I was the friend I had been waiting for. Inside me lived the friend and the contact with the whole that I had missed and been cut off from. A journey that has continued ever since. The door home had opened again, the contact with something greater within me had occurred and so it has continued to be. Our inner awareness is like the sky. That sky is the same as the infinity that embraces and surrounds us. Bowing to life and the mystery it is, is one of the greatest gifts we can give to ourselves.

This experience transformed my whole life. I had no words for what had happened, it has taken me almost thirty years to be able to write what I am putting into words here. All my so-called addictions or love substitutes just disappeared. For example, smoking just disappeared by itself. Drinking as well. Everything had been to fill the longing, the pain and the inner hole I had been carrying.

Thanks to the awareness, love and experience of wholeness and that nothing was missing me, I now experienced that I was divinely perfect. At home in myself and wholeness, free from the illusion of separation. All the addictions were replaced by presence, a loving one. I remember sitting every night to do my evening meditation of smoking in a conscious way. I had gotten into the habit of quitting smoking in a way that was loving to me. This habit, or habit, I got after my mother. Cigarettes had replaced love from her. I light a candle and slowly I will smoke lovingly. My love for life, mom and myself are all one. I sit with the cigarette. The hand but can not bring it to the mouth. The energy is not moving. I just sit in total harmony and know that from now on love and understanding will have replaced the cigarettes. It had, I never smoked again. It was just clear. I had no words for what had happened, it has taken me almost thirty years to even dare to put it into words. The whole universe lives inside me. The passion for my own life comes to life. All questions, all answers, all possibilities. Why has no one told me that this is possible? That this is who we are beyond thoughts and history. Beyond religions and philosophy of life. The one who is me is beyond time and space. In this book I call that quality our inner nature and/or buddha nature. It may sound big and strange when I write this and it really is, in a way. The experience of paradise, but in another way it is not. It is so simple and obvious. A few inches down from our head sits our heart. Not only the physical one, but also our spiritual one. When we open that door, we open ourselves to the whole universe. In my eyes, it's a human right for everyone to come home to themselves. From that day on, my life changed. I was no longer controlled or identified with the little girl who felt left out. I was free. This freedom and awareness meant that I never again identified with the story. Healing has continued and wounds have been allowed to come up to heal. But the one who sees and embraces everything has never left me. Awareness is everything and always will be.

The process made me see my thoughts and open my emotional memories.

I saw and I understood. There was only an acceptance of what had been. My heart had opened after being closed. I could see this little person who was me. Her unique journey. I could see how her mother had struggled in her unconsciousness and pain of not being wanted and loved. I could see how her father's pain had closed him in. I saw how everything was connected. What had been missing was an awareness. No one had been able to stop and look at what they were carrying. For me, the door of my heart had now been opened and with it the door was open to the whole and the divine. The silent still presence that constantly embraces. The experience of being one with the whole universe. That I am the meaning of life. Life wanted me here. I wanted me here.

To stop and face my inner self. To sort out and start taking my own feelings and experiences seriously. It gives space to start understanding that there is something more.

To let go of the old. To step out of the way of myself. To be able to see, feel and rest in the inner source of bliss. To be one with life itself. To find the passion for your own life. I wish that for everyone. It is awareness and only awareness that has set me free. When it is allowed to exist, all wounds can come to the surface and heal. All wounds are an opportunity to be reconciled, healed and transformed from pain to love. You can compare pain to the clouds in the sky and love and awareness to the sky. When we think we are the clouds separated from the sky, we live in a painful illusion of who we are. When we see and understand that the sky is who we are. The space where clouds can pass and disappear. When I had my experience, it was like I had rewritten, felt and dived straight into the cloud. Through the cloud I came out and discovered that the sky was there, the whole that had always been here. The cloud was my story. There may be clouds in the sky to this day that I dive into, but the awareness that the sky is always there and embraces does not disappear. There behind the clouds the sun shone. The sky is the awareness and the warming rays of the sun can be seen as the unconditional love that embraces us.

THE WAKE UP, MY HEART IS CALLING FROM WITHIN. IT HAS ITS OWN LONGING. GUIDING ME ONE STEP AT THE TIME IN DEEP DIVING AND TO EXPLORE. OLD PATTERNS LEAVING ME...

*T*he process that opened my inner doors was the greatest of gifts. I stopped, my heart opened. In that I started to meet my inner self. Starting to sort out and accept my story as it was. Starting to feel my own feelings. Standing on my side, not what someone else said I should feel or be. At the beginning of the process it had been difficult to remember but the memories came one by one through everything we did. Breathing exercises, guided meditations, writing, writing and writing about everything that I had brought with me from my history, everything that had been. When you write down your thoughts, feelings and experiences, you can start looking at them from the outside. An incredible help. The identification and all the mess I had on the inside became clear. With the help of all this, the journey took a more and more loving form in all the understanding and in all the connections I could see. After my experience of being the whole, stillness, trust and love became a tangible reality for me. So the journey I had made had gone from identifying with my thoughts, to starting to feel my feelings. To connect thought with feeling. For example, "nobody loves me", which had been one of my big basic thoughts. To feel how it felt, which was a lot of tears of sadness and anger. When an understanding took place, an acceptance came. The idea that I was not loved was no longer true. My experience after I finished crying was that I felt love for myself. I felt wanted and loved by life itself. It allowed me to look lovingly at my story. I could no longer blame anyone. No one had had more awareness or understanding than I had had before I began my inner journey. In it came an inner emptiness and stillness where I just was. Wonderful, quiet, whole and true! My life journey took a whole new shape. My relationship ended. It was no longer true to me. My job ended. Same thing there, it just ended because it wasn't where my energy was anymore. It reflected something old that I didn't need. Life took me by the hand and guided me into something new. Completely new, beyond what I knew existed. It was like the most natural process. Like when winter ends and spring comes. Everything was synchronised with the whole.

The meditations I learned during my transformation process were created by an Indian mystic who created them for modern Western man. I loved every millimetre of them. They both released energy and ended in total stillness and harmony. All except the morning meditation, which ended in dance to allow the energy to carry through the day.

A few months before the process began, I had felt drawn to a book that was in a shelving unit in a bookstore. I had bought the book with resistance and fear. Put it in my handbag and there it had remained. Obviously, I was not ready to open it. But during my weeks and months in this process,

I slowly realized that the book I bought, the meditations we did and the therapist we had, had the same source. That source was called Osho and was an Indian modern mystic. My heart knew something that 'I' was not aware of. My heart guided me, my heart and Osho were in contact.

Meeting him took me to a life beyond what I thought possible. In his presence I could sit and just be, in it I could continue to melt into wholeness, wisdom and expand into what was my true being.

I heard for the first time in my life someone speaking truths that I knew or felt were true. My whole being knew and relaxed. To feel this silent presence and that we are all one. It was so clear to me when I was in my own presence and experienced total togetherness. In an environment where every individual has the same intention, it becomes so much easier to feel and become aware. We were all truly like waves in the same ocean. Sitting in silence together makes the quality of silence so much stronger that you can almost touch it. The space that we usually forget about becomes the reality we merge with. To sit in this empty presence with someone who completely and totally just is. Having had that experience when he was in his body has made me know that that presence has always been there and will always be there whether he or we have any body for the energy to pass through.

I had been abandoned and betrayed by both my parents. That pain had taken me home into myself where an acceptance and reconciliation had happened and continued to happen. In that process, my heart had been opened and there lived a wisdom, power, like a fire, a longing that had its own way. A longing similar to the potential that lives in a seed. The energy and longing knows and finds its own way. I as "Lena" just disappeared. I was the awareness around and in me. I could only bow and step aside, give in and follow. I was no longer the one who knew. Everything that was happening was so much bigger than I could have ever imagined. The longing that lived in me and my mind was like a burning fire and power. A fire and energy I had locked away long ago and forgotten even existed. I was the one who saw and witnessed what was happening. Life took me to Osho. My first encounter with Osho had happened within me. I had no spiritual training or even any idea that this world existed. Meeting him was like remembering something I had put down and forgotten long ago. A modern mystic in our time. It is one of the greatest of gifts I have ever received. Sitting with him for the first time in person. There are probably a thousand people sitting in a large meditation hall. Everyone is in silence. Everyone is still and everyone closes their eyes. Osho who has come in is sitting quietly and he is also closing his eyes. This silence and this presence 'spoke'. It was magical. Here I was, an ordinary girl from Stockholm, not a seeker but someone who had just been given a new path to walk. Now here in this spiritual presence. How had I ended up here? It was not through my thoughts and old knowledge. It had happened in a way that was divine, wondrous and magical to me. As I understand today, it is the energy of a master that attracts the disciple. This made perfect sense to me. Now I sit here in wonder in a sea of other silent meditating seekers. Was I a seeker now? I did not feel like one. I felt more grateful and in wonder. Osho closes his eyes and I feel seen and loved for the first time in my life. A wonderful warmth and self-awareness fills me mixed with a great wonder. I just fall deeper into love with the mystery of life. Who could have imagined this. Silent tears of gratitude fall down my cheeks. I experience total love. A love beyond what I have ever known. That contact with Osho became my life. The contact with divinity got a frame, a mirror. Of who I truly am.

For the next seven years, I did everything I could to be in this conscious presence and wisdom.

I worked and sold what I had to have money and be able to immerse myself in this inner silent quiet wisdom. To be able to live so totally in awareness, in the present together with others is incredibly powerful.

I trained as an Osho therapist, which is based on a conscious presence. All his therapeutic meditations transform our energy. They take us away from our intellect and home in the present moment and our hearts. I was also initiated in various healing techniques. I travelled around the world for experience. The school of mysticism, the psychology of the buddhas, advanced counselling etc etc.. my thirst was big.

When Osho left his body in 1990, it was almost exactly seven years after the day I stepped into a basement room on shaky legs to stop and face myself. A little more than seven years since I stood there wondering if I should buy the book with his face on it. He left his physical body but his presence has never left. It is constantly with me in life.

Being with a master has many different levels. It is the reflection of your own divinity. When you meet a person who is empty and beyond identity, it is like a window opening to the sky. The inner divine sky. The Master can be seen as the window frame. As we have often closed the natural inner contact, this meeting can open that contact again. It is like when we fly up through the clouds. We see that there the sky is endless and ever blue. Something we may forget when the cloud cover is thick. To meet the energy that magically exists within us and has always embraced us. For me, that contact is a love affair with life and wholeness, the most important there is. All other love affairs are secondary. A meeting beyond time, form and space. I know nothing, but this contact is everything to me. It may be that all contacts that take place beyond words in love with a child, an animal, nature or a human being are equal in their filled emptiness. But with a master, our inner emptiness is illuminated. We know that we have thoughts and feelings. We have to learn to sort them out and reconcile them. But the spiritual aspect of us, the emptiness we all are, the living potential that lives within us beyond what we have learned. What is it? The silent still presence that we all know but may have become afraid of. A master illuminates the awareness and trust in life. That we are all perfect and that we are all the whole. That understanding or trust in the mystery of life comes into focus. A master is not in the place of you. A master can be a mirror for the divinity that lives within us. We have not been taught that knowledge. we have been taught to drive a car for hours, but to find trust in life and that we all have a loving inner potential or presence that longs to expand, we have never been taught that. As natural as for a flower to go from seed to full bloom. As magical as when a butterfly is born from its chrysalis, a flower bursts out, it is magical when we begin to live and affirm ourselves from the inside. Magical and at the same time completely obvious and simple. Osho with his presence and meditation techniques gave me the opportunity to live from the inside out.

Living for long periods in India was extremely valuable. It was stepping out of everything known and just letting yourself be lived from the inside out. A holistic experience that was so strong that we are all one. We were thousands of people from different backgrounds. We were there for one purpose, to meditate and expand into the present and the whole. And so we did. The evenings after the evening meditation where we all sat quietly and just listened and took in, were magical. The experience that we are like a big ocean where the waves rise up but are not separated from the sea. Each one of us is like the waves.

As a little boy, I never wanted to go home after being in India for a long time. But life and as I call it Osho, wanted to bring me out in life. Osho taught me with his presence that everyone is divine, that God lives within us. Stop and look. Everything is here for us and we are fully taken care of. He also wanted us to celebrate life and live it. Now the challenges would come by going out and coming home again.

Nothing else can be more important, as I see it, than to become aware of who we are and to learn to live our life in truth and harmony with our inner self. To allow ourselves to follow our heart and the wisdom that is within us. To live in harmony with what is. What became my path is bigger than what I ever imagined. I could never have even dreamed or wished for this as inwardly I did not know it was possible. I bow in reverence to the greatness that guides me and all of us.

To be able to live the life that is meant for me. To fully say yes and let my life be one with life's desire has given me such a sense of wholeness and joy.

Life Wanted Something From Me. Inner Wisdom And Potential Show The Way. From Thirty-Five To Forty-Nine. Living The Unknown Knowingly ...

*L*ife is amazing and constantly filled with surprises. When I started living from the inside out. Started following my inner voice, passion and creativity, life became a present and true adventure. An adventure that continues. Becoming aware and being able to share and give the energy that I was meant to give, it has created happiness and deep gratitude. I, who was once both shy and introverted, now had a whole new opportunity by sharing my insights. Life has a sense of humour. They give us the opposite of what we think. Now came a time to share by standing in front of groups of people. In total, I accepted the challenge in harmony with life itself. Even though I was vulnerable, there has always been an inner peace in everything I shared and did. A calm and a rest in the fact that what I have done has been in total harmony and true to me.

Just returned from one of my trips to India with the powerfully transforming presence of Osho, all the divine meditation processes, friends, therapists, all the zorbas and all the buddhas. To take the time to live in the strong presence and share the silence with so many other people was an incredible gift. A day in that presence was like three months or even longer at home. Each trip took me deeper into the stillness and the joy of just being. Then I get a phone call. It's Bengt Stern, the doctor who once advised me to begin my inner journey. He had retired as a doctor and had now started his own course farm, Mullingstorp. There he had the course "Meet yourself". He wanted me to come as he had a foreign therapist and doctor who would lead a permalink course of ten days. All his assistants and coworkers would be participants in the course, an extension of the course he himself had. Bengt, who had kept track of me and what I had done, thought I was perfect for the job as I had devoted my life to deepening my knowledge of our inner world and had attended many meditative therapeutic courses since we last met. The course leader needed an assistant and I became that assistant.

In all the years and all the trainings in therapeutic techniques, I had never thought once that I would work with this. All the trainings that came my way and those that I had money for I did. I never had a pile of money to draw from and I could start to see that when life wants something, it happens. Money comes and all the pieces fall perfectly into place by themselves. Looking back today on this time, I can only see how confidence guided. In my mind, the decision was already made, that I would live in harmony and in truth. To go with life. That life knows and I can naturally be guided. It is and has been a divine gift. I had been given the gift to rest within me. The longer an education was, the better for my own part. My love for the mystery and adventure of life became deeper, stronger and clearer. The strong presence that there was nothing else but to just be in this sense of wholeness together with others. To clear away all that stands in the way of a fully approaching life.

When I arrive at the course center, it turns out that the man I will be assisting and working with is a friend and therapist I met just a month earlier in India. He had never said he was going to Sweden and neither had I. We both come from Osho's meditation "school". I am happy to see him again and am struck by how perfectly life plans our lives. Gratitude fills my heart. We all play a perfect role in this theatre of life. The ten days are incredibly beautiful and I feel great confidence in the process he leads. This course was the opening for me to step out and start sharing what I have gained in the last seven amazing years.

A call comes shortly afterwards and I am offered to come and continue working at Mullingstorp Kursgård, which I initially struggle against. I had never thought of leading courses. I was shy and this was Bengt's course farm. Bengt was known for his slightly brash and controversial manner. He was an extremely strong person. He had been on an inner journey himself and understood the importance of working with people's inner selves. That we humans are existential and our energy as we are we need to live. That we need to meet ourselves, get to know ourselves, express what we carry and have put in. I was also asked to return as soon as possible to India, to Osho Resort to work there. It was like a door opened into a new phase of my life. At Mullingstorp, the courses were dynamic. Body psychotherapy was one of the tools used to find emotions, memories and patterns stuck in the subconscious. Bengt who compiled the "Meet yourself" courses became ill and I was asked to lead and bear some of the responsibility. The years I came to spend at Mullingstorp were an incredible life education for me. His hard aggressive way made me constantly question myself and find inner truths. It was an amazing school for me. I knew inside that I would be there. So there was never a questioning or a fight inside me. Just opportunities to grow, digest and understand myself deeper and deeper. Life is the school we go to and this was an extremely important part for me to be able to integrate and live from the inside out.

My years at Mullingstorp were intense and extremely instructive. Bengt got cancer in the beginning when I was there. Together with another doctor, I was asked to take overall responsibility for the course center. Bengt was a controversial person with many healthy thoughts about how we humans need to release our energy and feel our emotions to feel good. The course process he created before I arrived involved meeting oneself.

I took the responsibility and for six years I was there as the responsible course leader. They were fantastic years in many ways. We were among the first to work on this inner plane and the course center had its glory days. The importance of working with body psychotherapy, meditations, breathing exercises to open up old emotional memories. Emotional memories that have been in the subconscious and blocked the energy to be released. When we keep the energy locked inside us, it cannot flow in a balanced and healthy way. We are born as open divine beings, during childhood we shut down and not until we consciously begin our inner journey again do we release the life energy. This happens to all of us humans. The innocent energy of the child is found through the grace of making our inner journey on a conscious level. You who are reading this text right now have been given the grace to have that realisation. It is a gift that comes to us. I have many wonderful memories from that time. But I especially remember one incredibly beautiful and brave man. He was about sixty-five years old and had just retired. He had had a heart attack and had been hospitalised for it. Now he wanted to find out if his heart was more than just a pump that moved blood around his body. On one particular occasion, he held my hand tightly, "Lena, be here with me, in this breathing exercise. I feel I must find the answers within me, I do not want to die unconscious". He was and had been a businessman and leader throughout his life. He had been very successful and loved his wife who had been there for him but he had never expressed his gratitude. During the exercise we had, he went from experiencing the same pain as a heart attack, only this time it was an emotional attack. First came the fear, then the pain, it opened an endless source of love. A love he wanted to express to his wife but never could. Now it came and he cried, cried rivers, in my lap. He could hardly stay there for the next few days, he wanted so much to go home and tell his wife how he really felt. His heart attack in the destructive sense had become a spiritual attack where only love and togetherness existed. This work is worth everything. Don't know what happened to him after the course. But how happy and grateful he was when he went home was enough for me. That was payment enough. He had known by breathing. His understanding that his heart was holding back love. It was now released.

Bengt Stern, like many others, was a wounded little boy inside and he was a brave doctor. He dared to question and provide new alternatives to how a 'sick' person can heal himself. By stopping and facing his inner self and his feelings. Very brave as I see it. He understood that we carry emotional memories that must be released in order for the body's life energy to move freely. When it cannot, we become ill. That all diseases have their explanation. His courses were popular but for me it became clearer and clearer that I would no longer stay there as the main responsible and therapist. I could see clear reflections of my father's energy. That I would be there for him. That my value was never appreciated even though he was the one who was sick and needed me. I was poorly paid for the work I did and should be grateful that I was there. It was a leadership with underlying threats if I did not do a good job. I loved the opportunity to share but it got to a point where I no longer felt I could stand as a responsible course leader anymore. I wanted to quit and I did. Bengt got very angry and threatened me in various ways. He had always wanted me to be independent and not depend on him and Mullingstorp. There was a voice inside me that said it was time to leave. I have always followed that voice. It has been my security. If it says, jump in the river, I will do it. That voice is the one that knows something about me. From the outside, it may look like I don't know what I'm doing. I don't either. But trust and my inner self know.

So just as life had taken me by the hand and guided me there, life also took me by the hand and my time at Mullingstorp came to an end. It was time to take the next step. A step I did not know what it was. I just knew that now it was time. Then it turns out where to go next. Usually with a bit of a rest in between. When things are done, they are done. The energy is no longer there. From the outside, this can sometimes be difficult to relate to if you don't understand. Bengt was unfortunately both angry and disappointed that I left. He had other plans for me and my work there. I had to follow the path I had started on, there was no other option. In my heart I love Bengt for what he shared, created and believed in. It was he who once made me turn my gaze home and into myself. Thank you beloved Bengt for that.

I love freedom and stepping into the unknown and knowing nothing.

At this time I had a boyfriend who had a house in Italy, in Capri. He was going there and I could now go with him. A gift and such a beautiful place to meditate, nourish and just be. Now he and our relationship could have more energy and focus. We traveled some together to other places too. I took him to the Osho meditation center. He took me on a camel safari up in Rajasthan, India. A week out with three camels and two camel drivers. Walking with the camels in sandstorms and silence, an incredible experience. Absolutely wonderful that after years on a course farm and focus on others, the gift came to just take care of myself, enjoy the freedom of just being. Beautiful places that nourished the inner self. I have loved my life. To follow what is. To go with what wants to happen. To constantly see that life has taken me where I should be.

I had met Lars Knutsson on several occasions when I worked at a transforming retreat place.. I had been there during his process with the cancer he was suffering from, which made him stop and look home and into his own energy. Now he called me up and had bought a farm house up in the middle of Sweden.

"Hi Premleena, would you like to come and help me create a group transforming place.? I just bought a nice little house that my wife and I had planned to remodel. When can you come? We are working hard here with craftsmen". As I remember it, it didn't take many days before I was up there looking. What would the meditation hall look like? Where would it be? With two people with such flair, it wasn't difficult. Then came the next question. "Can you create a course to fill the course yard?". Of course my answer was yes. My heart was full and to share what has helped me transform my life is a gift to me. My and our goal was to create a unique course structure... not something that already existed. A vision that all people can have an opportunity to live their lives more lovingly. So my happiness to be this channel where structure and exercises were allowed to form in a perfect harmony. That the inner knowing created this whole beautiful process in three and a half days. To set the life energy in motion. To introduce Osho's meditation techniques that support the modern man to access his inner self. Learning to breathe and stay with your feelings. To see our history with guidance and be able to increase our loving presence beyond the idea of who we are. To say sorry and thank you to what is no longer helpful. To travel from the world of thoughts down into your inner self and feel your loving heart and share it with others. It became "door opening courses". I had again my inner guidance and feeling about what wanted to happen. At this stage in my life, I really gave it my all, and then some.

The years that followed were so incredibly valuable. They meant expansion, beyond what I didn't think was possible. It created a curation process that slowly grew and attracted people to stop and start their inner journey.

Lars was known from having trendy jeans shops in Stockholm, I was known in the inner " meet yourself" world. course, for example from Mullingstorp. Together with Lars and his new wife, Dalarna and Vikarbyn got a name on the world map. Baravara became known through TV and articles were written about me and us. Therapists who were old meditation friends from the time in India with Osho started working there. I led more and more courses. Door opening courses, The Work courses, Healing courses, different parts of the long "Training for life". During the six years I was there, everything was absolutely fantastic. There was no separation at all. It became my life to lead and work in a classroom... There was so much love for me even if there were also old patterns that haunted.

I was overjoyed to be given the space to create this course process. But after a few years, I realized that I was not part of the course farm. Plans and developments were not something I was part of anymore. This hurt me and slowly I realized that my exclusion was also here, albeit small. However, it was completely ok as I felt that this was the place for me. The courses filled up more and more, everything spun faster. When you give so much of yourself, it is extremely important to stop and fill up in small and large doses. I was happy and extremely appreciated. Lars Vedam Knutsson and his third wife and children, parents and his children were all involved in different ways. I wanted to be there for everyone. But I was never a natural part of their lives. In just being, yes, in the process, yes, but not in the family. That wasn't the intention either. But it hurt me at times.

To fill my batteries I often went to India and Osho Meditation Resort to be with myself. To refill, specially before the next course year starts. In India I meditated and met many of my old friends. I relaxed there, and one of the times I met a man and really "fell in love. A man comes with big steps straight into my heart. I was not fully prepared for that. We may never be. But me with my full course schedule. He living in America at the time, in California and Hawaii. Nothing that fitted into my Swedish group life. But the love and attraction had come and at first it looked like I would be able to include him in my life. He wanted to take new steps in his life. He came, I bought a house up there where we could live together, near the group place was… and he started to work with me. It didn't work out. After half a year I, we made the choice to leave Baravara and the life I had lived there. The deep feeling in my stomach guided me again. I was very tired after 23 groups a year for 6/7 years. An incredibly big but important step for me. But the tiredness inside me was great. And the love for the man even greater. Resting on the beaches of Hawaii was a gift. It was much needed. I had a strong feeling that it was of important to move and let go. To die into the unknown again.if I had stayed in the position I had at Baravara, the strong identity of being the "important group leader" it would have closed me in a role.

To allow me to love and be loved was a fantastic gift to start with. Travelling between Sweden and Hawaii. However, it slowly started to reflect too much of my "mom story". I had ended up in paradise again. My old story within me started to take over, projected to my partner, pain of not being wanted and loved was growing strong and life is becoming more like looking at old wounds than a love story with a happy ending. My patterns have come to the surface and I have only one thing to do, embrace them. In the midst of all the pain I see the gift of life, how can life present this situation so perfectly? That I could now see my story anew with more awareness and love. Healing could take place in depth. Thanks to awareness, connection and trust in life. Knowing that I am something infinite does not mean avoiding looking at the pain. It means being able to embrace it and let it melt like an ice cube in lukewarm water. That is what I had to do now. Hold the pain in my hands and let it melt. To ad to this I could only be there 3 months at the time so we where both tested with this longing, coming and leaving because of that.

Love is always a teacher. It came into my and his life. Nothing turned out as I had hoped and certainly not as he wanted either. It was what it was and healing had to happen. I was so sad. Just for your information, no more hard feelings from any of us. It was just not meant to be. I started to wright this book as my inner guided me to do.

In all the years I have worked with people, I have made several trips not only to India but also to USA. I met Byron Katie and trained in the Work, an amazing and obvious therapeutic technique. I was also in Sedona on several occasions to visit Osho's School of Mysticism. Trainings in the "Psychology of the Buddha's". Making time and space to constantly replenish and step out of the way for myself has been extremely important.

To have the opportunity to share the passion that my heart carries. To create freely from presence, wisdom, awareness and love. From the authentic source that lives within me. It is so infinitely great. I don't know how other creators do it. I think it's similar, when you paint a picture or create music. But for me, it was so incredibly big and beautiful when I created the process of the Door Opener or now Bliss courses and saw I can see how they affected every person who participated. I had a sense of what was to be created.. Not by me but through me. It was and am so clear. That something greater knows and guides us, step by step. For me, this wisdom became real and tangible through my years at Baravara and after that, still is. Even today, the courses roll with the same structure. It is here in the present that the intuitive wisdom lives. All the sessions I give are based on being totally present in the moment and intuitively *meeting* the other person or people who come. It is the only thing that can be done. Today I work with my retreats called " Bliss". Including all different parts that helps, my life wheel as a base so that we can all live our lives integrated, whole and open in a safe way.

For me, the joy of sharing, giving and allowing people to find their inner truth presence and energy has always been the focus. It feels like, the meaning of my life. But even if it is, it has been important to learn to set my own limits, to find the balance. My patterns from childhood have been strong. From pain and dysfunction into love trust and function. Helping and being there for my father, keeping his anger, pain and disappointments. My mother's absence and lack of desire for me. They could not do better but I can…. Only by living have the real insights become clear. Who, what is it that gives us all these gifts to see and understand the connections. Who, what is it that sees. To be able to see without judgment, to be able to live open and aware is a grace.

THE CHALLENGES OF LOVE AND THE AGE OF TRANSITION - THE PASSION FOR LIFE CONTINUES FROM FORTY-NINE TO FIFTY-SIX

*L*ove took me in many directions. As love does when we let it in. Many journeys became yours in both my inner and outer life. The love and infatuation I experienced was total and one of the most total I experienced in my life. I had to expand beyond what I thought was possible. We may think that love comes completely out of nowhere, but for me, each love carousel has taught me so much about myself. I have expanded and reconciled in my heart. Love opens new doors. The power of love makes it possible, otherwise we might just ignore it. This time it took me away all the way to California and Hawaii. Straight into a new paradise. Walking with my toes on a beach, eating fresh mango from the trees, not having a single moment to spare. Getting to meditate and be in love with my partner who has the most amazing house there. What a luxury. But love brought me back into myself on a deeper level. On the one hand, it took me into my old emotional memories. My mother who had lived, in my eyes, in paradise once before she died. The place in Indonesia that I got to visit. All these memories came straight up on the table. My longing for her, to have grown up without a family, mom or dad. For the last few years I had been living in a borrowed family, "just being the family". Now that it was no longer there for me, the pain came up for the mother who left me as a child. I had to embrace "little Lena", love her like no one else did yet again. I had been so focused on others for so long that I had forgotten and had no space for me. Love made sure that this was activated. How can life give us what we so desperately need? Or how we attract what we need to be whole. The man I met and fell in love with hoped I would want to look at his wounds and that together we could live and reconcile with what stood in the way. But he did not want that. He, as I perceived it, shut down more and more. A deep reconciliation work with him and my mother took place. The pain could be transformed into love. This time it took time but it was possible. Being aware or having experiences of not being our story does not mean we are 'done'. Rather, thanks to experiences of peace, wholeness, and total harmony, we can understand the vastness of clearing away old pains. Dare to stop and feel until it becomes clear. I could see that the truth was no longer the longing for my mother's love, but the truth was that I had longed for myself. Love for the man I met gave me opportunities to see many things. Love makes us whole. Maybe not in the way we think, but in the way we need. Life wants the best for us and always gives us what we need to grow and expand beyond what we think. Everything we receive is of the highest value. When we live with life's challenges instead of fighting against or dwelling on the fact that it 'shouldn't have happened', the realisation and trust that life is totally loving and caring for us beyond what we can comprehend comes.

Our relationship had potential and great energy, but it didn't work out. The relationship ended.

I traveled home to find a peaceful place to meditate. It was with an old friend who leads meditation retreats around the world. She lives in India up in the Himalayas with her Indian husband. For a month I let the stillness and silence embrace me. Not a word for three weeks. With sadness in my heart. Without the identification with my job at Just Be, door opening courses or love, the presence in the emptiness became very strong. A gift to myself. It is so easy to get caught up in different identities and identifications. When we do that, we only create more and more pain. We fight with what is and would rather have what was. When we accept deeply, the trust in the presence that everything is as it should be increases. Even if we take a few trips into the world of emotions, which is needed to let go deeply, there can be a clarity and understanding that embraces the whole situation. I, with my history, have needed a lot of time to embrace all the old emotional memories.

To go with the flow of life. Saying yes to the gifts and challenges that come my way. Responding to the needs of my body. Being a woman and facing the so-called transitional age. It has had its challenges but to live with what is happening and listen to the cleansing that wants to happen in the body after a 'long' life. I have completely and fully let my body have its process. Let all the old memories around sex and menstrual cycles come to the surface and go away. Let the thoughts that have come and stood in the way be embraced. This is a natural part of life. I can only face and deal with it as lovingly as I possibly can. Within me there is no age. With every step that takes place and is new, I feel like a curious child. Like a child on a journey, open and curious.

EVERYTHING IS HAPPENING AS IT SHOULD! EXPANSION INTO THE UNKNOWN. WE ARE LIKE A FLOWER THAT CONSTANTLY SEEKS TO GIVE THE UTMOST.

*A*t fifty-six, I took writing seriously. I had long tried to repress and avoid the challenge. Now I felt pregnant with something that had to come out in a writing creative process. I knew in my mind that now is the time. When I am almost done with it, the next step in giving sessions and trainings can happen, or if life wants something else. Maybe more books may be written what do I know at this point. Life continues to happen. I am here allowing myself to be a channel for the loving and divine energy of life. We cannot do anything about how our lives begin. But through understanding, acceptance and reconciliation, we can have the quality of life we long for and end this life in the dignified and loving way we desire. We can control and have power over that. In my case, I have accepted and reconciled with my history. No longer living in any separation with it that it should or would have been any other way. Through divine support and insights, I have learned to live more lovingly and consciously present. Based on wholeness from the inside out. To constantly surrender and rest in what is. Everything else creates pain, war and separation.

We are all channels for this life energy. The only problem is that we take it personally. We think we are the ones doing it. We try to control instead of being open and trusting what is happening. The universe and life is an incredibly loving place. Maybe we should learn through our challenges. When we look beyond the thoughts and ideas, perhaps we can see and understand that this journey of life is a gift.

To live open and present so that life can flow freely. That is my task. In it, I can face life, myself and what is beyond.

How can life get better than this? I don't know. I don't know. It's perfect just the way it is. By not being away at work but working a lot from home, I have had the opportunity to just be in the free flow. Able to follow what is. In recent years, I have been given the gift of sharing my life with a child, the most divine of gifts. For me, who never had children of my own, has now been allowed to exist with all unconditional love for her. A great gift with all its challenges.

As long as I am here, I will continue and live in the confidence I have. To be true to myself fully. To act and let live what wants to be lived. To be open and to receive. To give everything, to be true to myself. To give and share life energy, replenish and be still. knowing that everything happens as it should. Maybe not always as I imagined, but better. Seeing only the parts and not the whole, I can only enjoy what is happening. On the inside, there is no age and on one level I feel as in love with life as I have always been. I feel young, like a girl and I feel old and wise, absolutely wonderful. To continue this divine adventure with life's experiences.

I remember what my father once said to me when he got old. "Lena, it's not so easy to get old. All your friends just become less and less of themselves. But Lena what I see has happened to you since you started your inner journey is different... It's that you are becoming more and more of the little girl I once saw running around at home. I love to see that. It's probably too late for me to become more of me. But I feel like I'm being sucked along behind you somehow". This stuck with me. To let yourself grow and become more of yourself throughout your life. Not shutting down. My dad said he didn't understand what I had gotten myself into. Maybe not intellectually but emotionally he did, intuitively.

As a woman of fifty-six, a lot happens in your body. The hormonal journey that has been going on since adolescence has now come to an end. The body is changing quite a lot, it is no longer attractive in the same way as before. But as I experience it much more pleasant to live in. I have welcomed the body's process and not wanted to disturb the natural order. This has deepened the inner connection in a much more natural way. To live and feel the love and wisdom that lives here within me.

I have never been rich on the outside but I have always felt rich on the inside. I want to continue to rest in that richness and share it with others. I openly accept what life wants. I love simplicity and I love freedom. Freedom for me is to continue to follow my heart and what is true. Today, my mom and my story are just total acceptance and love. There are emotional memories that can live in different situations. But it is just another opportunity to digest and become more whole. The story is within me not outside. I just needed that mom and that dad. This story to be able to sit here today and feel at peace with everything. Life is a never ending journey. With body and a day beyond it. Loving life, oneself and others is built on an understanding, an awareness, nothing else.

Life is so exciting and constantly presents new challenges.

I love life, it is my passion. And I feel that life is holding my hand in the most amazing way. Following the inner still, silent voice and the guidance that constantly embraces me. It is like a quiet silent prayer within me. With awareness it is possible. In awareness we are in paradise wherever we are. Unconsciousness is pain and separation, wherever you are.

To live in harmony with what is. On the inside as well as on the outside. I feel so incredibly rich. Not on an external level but on an internal one. I feel whole and filled with just being. An inner richness that has always existed and will always exist. A richness where creativity originates, inner longing and potential exist. A richness that is vibrating love energy beyond all forms. Early in life, I knew that external wealth did not attract me. Which then scared me. What is wrong with me? But the more insights and awakenings that have occurred, I can see that my whole being has longed to be able to live from a completely different energy, conscious and present. To live what has always been and will always be. Beyond illusions.

When I look back on my life, it may seem as if there was a plan, that every step was planned. But that has not been the case. Life is living itself, one step at a time, and that can only be understood when we stop and look back. That is what I am telling you here. We are not the doer. It may seem that way. But when we look and become aware, we see that it is the energy and life itself that lives us. It's exciting! To start seeing and understanding. Life is as it is. If you are reading this book, there is probably a longing within you to live a truer life. To clear up your misconceptions and old emotional memories. To step out of the way of life itself.

The body has its process, life has its process and who are we in all this? When I look at myself in the mirror, I can see that the body changes but the one who sees is the same, the one who has always existed. The one who sees without judgment. The one who sees that we have woken up in the morning, the one who sees that we have had a dream. We are the presence that sees.

A SUMMARY

*A*s a child, before I started to shut down, I was happy and in touch with life, divinity and myself. There was a natural and obvious trust. Then I started to shut down, I became more and more unconscious and the contact within me disappeared. Through events and interpretations in my childhood came sorrow and sadness. An identity that I was not wanted, not loved, or that everything that had gone 'wrong' was caused by me.

This meant pain and a life where I myself was not in the picture. I was controlled and unaware of my history. Unaware of the grief I carried. A grief that had become my identity. When I stopped and looked inside myself, the awakening and the truth came. I had dived straight into my sadness. The sadness that had been my identity was no longer true. Nothing had been my fault, nothing was mom or dad's fault either. What happened was that awareness made me free to see and understand. It is awareness that makes us free. But to understand it, we need to embrace and go straight into all the misconceptions and emotional memories we carry. Only through that did I find the truth about me. A work in progress. To openly truthfully and totally examine who I am. That who I am in truth is something never separated from the whole. I was and am whole, vibrating creative loving energy. My mom had been unaware of her pain, my dad as well. However, my father told me a few months before he would die, he was then eighty-three years old and our brief meetings came to be about life and death and my questions about how he felt inside, a form of loving reconciliation and understanding of each other. "Lena, I understand nothing of what you do or what you have found in your life. But I see that you are the only person I know who is becoming more of himself. You have come back to being more like the little girl I once saw as something divine, alive and beautiful. It is as if I am traveling with you in some form, as if in a boat's wake. I don't understand but feel that it is precious to me". Beautiful words and wonderful confirmation to hear. It's true that the energy we all carry attracts events on the outside. So the more we clean up and reconcile, the more light, possibilities and love we attract. That's what my father had felt. That there was more love and light inside me. I was no longer identified by pain and the sadness I had previously carried.

When I opened up within myself to what was true, life turned out to open up completely new paths and possibilities. Beyond what I previously even knew existed. Life is a mystery beyond what we can see and understand. Saying yes, trusting and being able to live in harmony with our inner self and life is a tremendous blessing. To be friends with yourself and life, letting awareness show the way. As we often only see the parts and do not have the awareness of the whole. To walk this life in trust and harmony. It is not how we start this life that is the point, but it is how we choose to live and how we want to end this life. You have an opportunity to influence that. For me, there are only two things that are important and that is, awareness and love. Awareness gives birth to love and love gives awareness. Like two wings on a bird. These two make our lives a wonderful journey and adventure. My vision of life is to trust my inner self and life. To be alive and live true from within my heart. I breathe in every moment and take in what is.... On the inside, I will always be the little girl who openly and in true wonder lives her life in trust and lets herself be followed by the love and longing in my heart.

WHY ARE WE AFRAID TO MEET OUR SELF. IT IS THE GREATEST GIFT.

"Truth is not to be found outside.
No teacher, no scripture can give it to you.
It is inside you and if you wish to attain it,
seek your own company.
Be with yourself".

OSHO

I often hear from people that they are afraid to look back. My answer is usually the opposite. The fear is when we don't look back, when we can't see or understand who we really are. The only thing that can happen when we stop and become more aware of who we are is that we experience more and more harmony, love, creativity and rest within us. We become happier and dare to be more alive, loving and creative. The only thing we encounter are thoughts and feelings. When we understand that, the space we are beyond that will be filled with pure presence which is who we really are. When we don't see and are aware, it's like driving a car with our eyes closed. Then we keep the handbrake on and accelerate at full speed, wondering where we are going or why nothing happens.

We all come from the same source of universal perfect energy. The one I told you about when I was five years old. The free flow from the inside out. We lack nothing. We are already perfect, free and one with the source we come from. Water should water, you should be you. As humans, we can increase our awareness of who we are. It seems if you look out at our planet that we are the only race on Earth that is so at war with ourselves. We have taken on the role of the one who has the right to take and consume resources without looking further than our nose. We do not see this whole perfect existence as a perfect creation but we have put ourselves on high horses and think from a perspective of unconsciousness. We cannot see the whole, it is not in our power. But what is in our power is to take care of the individual that is you. To with awareness stop and up and start opening the qualities of the heart again.

We will grow old if we live. The question then is how we want to live this life. If the longing is to live more peacefully, harmoniously, more lovingly, creatively, balanced in presence with yourself and life. Yes, then it is possible. All those qualities are already within you. They are waiting for you to be lived.

As humans, we share certain characteristics. For example, we all have THOUGHTS. Thoughts that come and go. No thought is personal, even if we hold a thought as personal truth until we examine it. Or thoughts that have come to stay and with which we have begun to identify ourselves. Thoughts that have interwoven and become like a shield or identity around and for us.

Often we have inherited them or taken the thoughts unconsciously as a survival strategy. The thoughts themselves have no energy but what they do to us when we hold them without examining is that they prevent us from being alive, present, free and flowing.

Thoughts can be likened to the shell around a seed. Whatever we write on the shell is not the energy or potential that is in the seed. If we write, paint and cover the shell with rose pictures, it is not the same as when the seed bursts open and starts to grow and become the wonderfully beautiful rose it is meant to be. The real rose has a process in itself where the scent, the color, the shape is unique.

All of you who love nature and its various forms. The stillness and peace that prevails when everything is allowed to take its course, naturally, simply and obviously.

Starting to see what we think about ourselves, others and life is extremely valuable. To be able to see them, to relate to them. Are they true for us now? To begin to see and examine what are the thoughts I have as an identity. Are they true for me?

We as humans share this with thoughts, we have certainly had the same thoughts many many times. Thoughts flow freely around us. We have to be careful not to take in any thought that we really don't want.

Thoughts have the natural ability to separate us.

Some examples: You are good, I am bad. I should be faster than I am. The train should be on time. The weather should be different. My partner should understand what I need. The children should be asleep now.

Etc etc.

When I think that my partner should be different, for example, these thoughts create a separation between us. If he or she also thinks like that, it becomes difficult to meet. You don't even meet yourself by thinking. Thinking takes you away and out of stopping here and now and investigating in depth. If I think that I am too fat and my partner should understand what I need. We live in a dream world within ourselves. When we stop and start to relate, can see bad it says I have some choices to make. Right now how do I want to relate to my body? What do I want with my partner? How can I meet my needs, how can I communicate them etc.

All thoughts separate us from ourselves and the world around us. Thoughts are not the problem, but the fact that we do not see them or have become attached to them is. We need to see what separates us from the truth and the now that is.

We should not fight our thoughts, we should start to understand them. Get a relationship with them in a healthy way.

If we have long been identified with them, we should really look at them in a loving way and examine what the truth is right now. Thoughts are thoughts.

Becoming aware of what we think is extremely important in order to see who we are beyond them.

Another important characteristic we share is FEELINGS. They are related to the thoughts we have about ourselves. If we think a thought, we can examine how it feels. Feelings can be locked up and accumulated over many years from childhood onwards. We all have feelings. If they are locked up inside us, they are like water frozen into ice. When we begin to embrace them lovingly, they melt and the energy can flow again? All emotions are energy and have the same source within us. All trapped emotions that we have not felt clearly live within us and we can open up to them here and now. While thoughts have a way of separating us from the present moment, ourselves and each other, awareness of our own emotions can create empathy and compassion. By understanding my own feelings, I can understand how others feel. If I stay closed off, it can be difficult to empathize with others. In our modern society, we find it difficult to relate to emotions. We do almost everything to avoid feeling them. We escape in all kinds of ways just because we haven't learned that it's okay to feel. To start owning your own feelings and understand them. Not blaming others for your feelings. But start to deeply own, feel clearly and understand its source. Feelings are felt, otherwise it remains as unredeemed energy inside. As I wrote, it becomes like encapsulated ice, the energy cannot flow. Many people believe that it is dangerous to feel their emotions. Which we can believe if we have stopped and turned off. But it's not feeling them that's the problem it's fighting them that is. As we begin our inner journey and face ourselves, it is loving to have the outside support of someone who is aware of what it means to start seeing yourself.

Thoughts and feelings come and go. But there is a quality within us that is not separate. It has never come and gone. It is our ability to be in the NOW. It is in the present that I can begin to see and examine who I am. When I take that step, there is an acceptance and a witnessing. When I can see a thought and the feeling that comes with it, I have something to relate to. If I stop and see that perhaps the Bode thought and feeling comes from previously unresolved events, the person who sees it is bigger than the event, thoughts and feeling. It means that you are no longer identified.

The more we can see, understand and become aware of, the more love we experience.

It is as we take both thoughts and feelings to heart where an acceptance can take place leading to a life beyond separation.

In our HEART lives the whole, there is no separation. When we open the door into ourselves, we experience who we are beyond thoughts and feelings. Our hearts are like the sky, the space that embraces all the clouds. When we look closer, there is no cloud. When we begin to explore within ourselves who we are, there is no limited self. The heart gives us that wisdom. The presence that lives there has no time and space. Just like when we fall in love. Everyone talks about love but few really dare to feel and live that energy. It lives in all of us but most often we have put hurt feelings from childhood and up to different types of relationships around love. Then encapsulated with thoughts of how it should be and not be. When we see that and open up again, you will experience how the loving life energy fills you again. Here lives the wholeness. Here lives the ability to reconcile. To see that nothing has ever been broken. We have only turned off.

When we stop and see one of our thoughts, go down into the feeling and begin to examine what is true for us here and now, there is a sense of acceptance followed by a loving stillness. It just is. The truth within us has no moral aspect. It has more to do with an inner compass. When I am in touch with my inner self and true to myself, I feel good. When I shut down and run away from my own feeling, it hurts inside me. Of course, it depends on how much and how long I do it. But the principle of shutting out your own unique experience hurts. Being open and true to oneself is experienced as harmony on the inside. This is not something I made up, it just is. I have tried for thirty years to live as true as I can and I know how it feels when I do not. Not only me but also all the individuals I have met over the years who are beginning to understand the importance of becoming friends with themselves and understanding what it means in terms of well-being and presence.

It is not an ego trip to understand oneself, it is the opposite. The ego is in the thoughts, in the illusion we have about ourselves and life. When we start to look beyond it, we discover a whole new inner wonderful world.

We all have our UNIQUE journey here on Earth. There is only one of you. We all have our unique story. When we examine our story and allow ourselves to grow out of it, we create roots, opening the door to the truly unique expression that can only come through you. The fragrance that only you have. The creativity that comes from within your inner source. Only you can step out of the way of yourself so that the fountain of energy that lives within you can have its unique expression. That expression does not come from the world of thoughts but from an inner intuitive source. This source lives within each of us. We can only see it by stopping and sinking into ourselves through thoughts, feelings, in an accepting embrace of ourselves. Experiencing the loving stillness that naturally exists within us. Through that, the layers of inner unique passion and creativity are opened. We are all meant to be here on earth for as long as we are. What you choose to do with that time is up to you. If you choose to let a silent inner yes! to yourself and life sink in. No doing is needed, just a willingness. In that willingness, everything happens as it should.

Maybe it does, but we are not aware of it and maybe we spend our energy fighting against what is.

When we completely step out of our own way, our inner energy can fully guide us.

We all come from the same divine SOURCE and we will all return there. That source, that presence is our true nature. The one beyond all limitations. The quality that sees, always has been and always will be. To let our inner being just get our attention. To be able to stop here without any identity. To rest unlimitedly in this now.

ENERGY

It is so obvious to me that we are energy, inside and out. The energy that lives in every cell within each of us. We call it, tao, chi divine, consciousness or as I have chosen to call it here our inner source, life passion from our innermost. The energy can be compared to the life potential that exists in every seed. Every day I experience how the energy knows and the day happens by itself and is absolutely perfect. It is really not me who 'does' but it is the energy and life itself that knows. To follow the flow and flow with it. In it happens what should happen. A total harmony prevails. But it happens by itself from within. I can think a lot of things that I should do. But that doesn't help, because the energy doesn't live in the thoughts. The energy lives within me and that's where life works.

If life is the sea, then we are the waves where there is no separation from the sea. We are one and the same. The power of the sea makes the waves. If we can see ourselves as part of the whole and learn to live in harmony with energy, we live more lovingly and truly.

Energy moves and it has its wisdom. Quietly, sometimes more hastily. Learn to live with the sea. Let go and let go of fear. Learn to swim, live beyond control and the idea that you know how life should be. Let the energy and adventure of life guide you.

Our life energy has its unique journey. To be able to trust and learn to live with it. To feel that you are living your life. That the energy within you knows its truths.

To dare to let go. To include what is and not fight against it. Learning to live with the changes that happen. To understand within ourselves who we are. Learning to see the thoughts that pass, daring to feel our feelings. Be able to accept what is. Then the energy is transformed into pure love.

In that love lives an energy that is unique. The unique energy that only you have. When it is allowed to live, we can begin to rest in a stillness and peace that lives within us. A stillness and peace that is everyone's potential and divine life energy.

Everything we have around us in life is energy. The Earth is spinning and it is alive. Trees, plants and animals are alive and have their journey. We humans are also alive beyond what we think and understand. Just look at our bodies, alive and doing their part to keep us alive. Every part of the energy is doing its job. Every cell is doing its job.

If you look at our inner self as a seed, the thoughts about who we should be are the ones that hold the energy, like the shell around the seed. Emotions are the power and energy inside the shell. The desire to burst open is the love within us. The flower we will become is unique and that energy is within you. It is unique, each one of us is unique. And the invisible force behind it all is the invisible mystery of the universe.

This life energy that we all are, is in harmony with the whole and it has its own wisdom. A wisdom much greater than that which is learned in us. For many years I played and experimented with myself and the energy we are, in different ways. I love life, I love to be part of this mystery and I am mostly friends with myself and life. I live with the energy, not against. Sometimes, when life doesn't want the same as me, I can have a conversation with the whole about how I see the situation. But it is always me who has to give in, life wins. Loving what is can sometimes take a while, but most of the time I simply live with it. And it's amazing to see how everything falls into a harmonious pattern. We all belong together. And the more we step out of our own way, the more we dare to be open and let life and energy lead us, the more harmonious we are. From controlled chaos and organisation to living as one big harmonious organism. Where every part has its meaning and task.

We are the whole, not the parts. Like every drop of water that carries the saltiness of the whole sea within it.

Energy moves between poles like a river has two banks. Waves go in and waves go out.

Like a pendulum swinging from side to side, energy moves.

When we accept and allow unity to be our reality, we experience love.

Being identified with the parts and only one side creates "fight". Seeing the whole creates a sense of living with life which creates harmony. One moment alert, the next tired. One moment hungry, the next full. To be creative one day, then feel emptiness and be able to rest in it. Finding harmony in the natural movement of life.

When we don't see that we are the whole, we tend to project different parts onto other people, what we don't want to 'own' ourselves. We often do this in our relationships. Most often, unfortunately, we want to see ourselves as the good one and our partner as the bad one, or the one who is wrong. Or we do the opposite. The partner is always the one who is good, right and wise while you are the one who is wrong. We get stuck in one polarity. The truth is that everything exists and lives within you.

Keeping the energy in your body alive and moving is important. Examining our thoughts and making sure they are not stuck in old thought patterns, because that usually doesn't make us feel good. To dare to feel our feelings. To become clear and reconcile with old hurt feelings. Then life energy can have space and fill us with its loving presence. There is a Chinese proverb that says we grow old when our spine stiffens. It can be translated as we become old when we are stuck in old thought patterns. When we do not dare to live and realize our dreams or longings.

Learning to listen to the silence between and beyond thoughts and emotions. To allow the energy within you to live naturally and have the freedom to live and move.

It is not how life start that is the point… it is how you choose to live it now.

Polarities are needed for there to be movement. All polarities are interwoven opposites.

High - Low
Male - Female
Active - Passive
Work - Celebrate life

Being alone - Being together
The present - Longing
The waves go in and the waves go out
Open - Closed
Conscious - Unconscious
Happy - Sad
Strong - Weak
Pain - harmony

ABOUT TRUST

$\mathcal{W}$hen it comes to trust, it is important that we understand ourselves and life. Most often, we outsource trust to another person. We want to have trust in our partner, in friends or in authority, etc.

We can only trust ourselves and our inner nature. True trust in life. Trust in what is.

To gain confidence in yourself, you need to understand and know yourself. To gain confidence in life, we need to understand the natural flow and laws of life.

In my case, the confidence came when I started to understand myself, from my awakening onwards. Who I was and what I was carrying. Confidence came when I realized that who I was was the part that was empty, free and not identified with the past. The part that is in harmony with life and the whole. Trust in my inner self and in life went hand in hand. When there was no longer any separation.

If we do not trust ourselves and life, it is difficult to allow change in our lives. We then hold back the natural evolution that wants to happen. If we want a change that is lasting, we need to add awareness and love that is of higher value, more awareness. We cannot "take away" something unless we feel we are getting something else in its place. Trust is needed for change and transformation to be possible and a natural part of being a living human being.

When I start a work, individually or in a group, I make it clear from the beginning that we are not going to take away anything, but we are going to add. Adding more understanding, with more understanding comes more love. In that awareness and love we can increase our presence and transformation happens by itself. Change, transformation and expansion are natural. Trying to control and keep the energy in the same form is almost impossible. It takes all the energy to fight against instead of flowing with.

When I started my journey in awareness, I was a smoker. I smoked quite a lot and didn't enjoy it at all. I saw that smoking was connected to feelings I had with my mother. She smoked and loved to do it. It was pretty, sensual, socially good in her world. So when I came to her after graduation and got to spend time with her, it was a given that I would smoke too. It was something we in silence had in common. It was also a way to keep my emotions in some kind of control. When I started to see the bigger picture, I had a choice. Did I want to continue like her? A longing to be able to love her for who she was without having this attachment around smoking being our love bond. I started smoking each cigarette more consciously, more in the presence of myself. This took some time and became a form of meditation for me. I allowed my love for her to exist in my heart. I allowed love to exist for myself. The result was that I smoked less and less without any war within me. One day I didn't smoke at all and it has continued like that. The presence transformed the behaviour. This took maybe six months or so. The process of replacing, in this case smoking, with presence, love and understanding in increased presence and awareness. I saw the thoughts I had about smoking and I could feel the emotions that were there around my mother. The trust in myself, the trust that awareness, presence and understanding lead me to a greater loving presence.

My whole life changed when I started my inner journey. Everything in my outer life fell away by itself. It no longer helped me. My job as a clothes buyer fell away. It was replaced by other jobs where I could be free and travel. To later work with raising presence, awareness and love in people's lives. My relationship fell away and was replaced by a relationship with myself. Of course, I have had love relationships after that. I love the men who have come into my life. But I love the relationship with myself too. Friends disappeared further and further away and new ones came into my life. A web of loving connections around the planet, like a spiritual family. I became and am becoming truer and my life became and is becoming truer. All this by finding trust in my inner self and in life. You can find trust in you and in life.

If we all start to live our own power and follow it, respect for each other will be so much greater. Instead of me living in a way that I think you want. Or you living in a way you think your partner wants and your partner living in a way his or her mom wants etc. It becomes confusing and messy. It becomes a life built on assumptions about what others want and no trust.

CONFIDENCE IN YOURSELF

*W*e rarely learn about ourselves. Who we are as people. That we have thoughts, that we feel, that we have an inner potential and possibility within us. That it is possible to listen and follow the unique life energy that lives within us. That trust in yourself is a possibility. To be able to trust, it is extremely valuable to be aware of who we are on the inside. To gain an understanding.

Our nature from the outside in can be seen like this:

First come our thoughts. They are like the shell around us.

We often find it difficult to see and become aware of our thoughts. But it is important to be able to do so. Thoughts are like a shell that can trap life energy. When we see the thoughts, we can start to examine whether they are true for us in the present. Are they yours or have you inherited them from someone else? By nature, thoughts are not ours, but they are like birds flying freely. When we have thoughts that lock us in, it's as if we believe in something we haven't investigated. Thoughts that are allowed to be free are like birds flying freely in the sky. Free, then thoughts and information can come to us that we previously had no contact with. When we start to investigate and get to know what we are thinking, the shell opens and the next level of energy comes to the surface.

Inside the shell are the emotions. In our lifetime, we have little understanding of emotions, which is a big mistake. Emotions have their own wisdom. They give us depth and take us back to the child we once were so that understanding and healing can happen. They give us a depth and are an energy that is natural and important.

But if there are thoughts that emotions are dangerous and that we need to control them, which means not feeling them, we are trapping our life energy and then the thoughts can become dangerous to us. Thoughts that keep energy trapped make us live in separation from ourselves, our inner self.

As children, we have emotions naturally. They are our means of expression before intellectual understanding comes.

When we were children, we felt our emotions and at different times we might have been told "don't feel that way" or "don't cry now" or "don't be sad about this" or maybe there was no one to see your feelings. Maybe anger was ugly. That's what was happening to me. I was filled with emotional memories that I had stuffed down and forgotten I was carrying at all.

When we start to open up to our feelings and the memories that are there, it can sometimes only take a few minutes of presence with the feeling and it becomes clear. Emotions are energy like a circle. When we get stopped in the middle, it's like the circle doesn't get completed. When we meet the emotional memories in presence and awareness, it is as if the other half is allowed to come along and the energy becomes clear. We release our energy and the experience of peace and freedom is the result. When I fight against feeling, it becomes a struggle between what is and the thought that I should not feel. The most natural thing is to become aware and feel what I feel in total acceptance. Feelings are natural. We need to become aware so we can embrace and receive them in a healthy way. Bring both the thoughts and the feelings home to our heart where they can be let go and go away.

When we accept our feelings and feel them fully step by step, we end up with a sense of oneness. A feeling of not being in separation with ourselves. The feelings, when accepted and experienced by ourselves, take us home to our hearts where our inner potential and energy reside. We are all unconditional love. It can come to the surface when we open the door to our inner selves and dare to see and feel what stands in our way.

The love that lives inside us, the unconditional love. It is natural to feel and live in the unconditional energy of love. We all have it. We all are it.

It is more natural to live in unconditional love than to fight against our whole inner nature.

When we feel our heart and the love that resides there, our unique qualities and unique nature come out more and more like a flower that has its own expression. It is the same for you.

In our heart lives the possibility of transformation. It happens when we embrace memories, emotions, events and just let total acceptance prevail. It can happen when the heart is open and with that comes reconciliation. The wisdom of your heart is in touch with the heart of every human being. Opening your heart to be able to know yourself, to look at life, to see others through the non-judgmental energy that is love.

Deeper into ourselves, we can rest in the place and quality that is still and quiet. The place that is unique in us. The place in us that is beyond all ideas and concepts of who we should be. A place where our unique essence vibrates. Our unique energy does not reside in our intellect but in our hearts.

There we vibrate with divinity. That which vibrates in harmony with the whole universe. All intuitive wisdom lives here. The whole lives in you.

You experience confidence in yourself when you understand and can see yourself. Your thoughts. Feel your emotions. Experience the love in your heart. Let your own unique potential be expressed. And rest in your own inner center. There lives stillness, wisdom in total presence. That place in you is also in total harmony with the whole universe.

From thinking you, to knowing you. Trust to feel the love in you and to just be yourself.

Unconscious thoughts and unresolved emotional memories are like a grain of sand in the eye. It prevents us from fully seeing and experiencing the present.

When you get to know your inner nature, you can trust your inner self and the silent voice and inner wisdom that lives there.

Be able to see the thoughts, explore and be able to let them go.

Feel and be able to see emotional memories that are there.

Dare to open your heart to yourself.

Be present and see your unique qualities.

Allow yourself to rest in your own quiet inner center so it can expand.

ABOUT ME WHEN TRUST BROKE AND THE BUTTERFLIES CAME.

A little after I started working at Mullingstorp's course center, after the first course I had only assisted on, I received a phone call early one morning. It was from a Norwegian woman who had attended a course. She wondered if I would consider working on a project in Tromsø in northern Norway. Of course, my answer was. My money was tight and I had spent the summer wondering how I would survive. I had been to wonderful friends on the west coast and plagued them with my worries. As both of them are conscious and loving individuals, they just let me carry on. "It will all work out. It always has for you" said my loving friend and her husband.

Then the call came. The caller said briefly "I'll ask the consultant who will lead the process to call you. Goodbye!" It was about six o'clock in the morning and I had not really kept up. No call from any consultant came and the weeks passed. For a while I thought I had made it all up. I called the woman back. "Did you call me or did I just make it up?" She had called and soon after Kjell, the consultant, called.

"Well, I guess we'll be working together. Can we meet this weekend? I'm in Oslo, can you come?" Everything happens perfectly and as a whole. I meet Kjell and we book all the dates for the project. It's now the end of August and in September we will start.

I travel up to Tromso. I feel like I am going to the end of the world. I have feelings of alienation and I feel vulnerable. Haven't quite gotten used to the idea. At Tromso airport, we meet later in the evening. At eight o'clock I arrive. Kjell with assistant Stefan should arrive around ten o'clock in the evening. Sitting alone and waiting. Not a person I see. Apparently not many flights land here. I have to sit in a bar that is closed. It is shouted out over the loudspeakers "Can Lena Wettergran come to the information?" This happens before everyone had cell phones. Kjell is late and will not arrive until after midnight. Knowing that most of my friends at this time are on their way back to India to be there for the fall and winter. I alone here and no one comes, then I fall into tears and feel like the most lonely person on earth. My patterns from childhood come up inside me. God does not want me either. That's why he sent me to the farthest corner of the earth, to just sit here. When everyone else is going to India together and meditating, dancing, crying and feeling total togetherness.

It may sound strange or childish. But that's how it was for me. Trust was not at its peak. Kjell finally arrived and we started the project, which would last for a year. Every six weeks we would meet, five days at a time. Up in northern Norway, it can sometimes be difficult to understand what they say when you are not used to it. I was also Swedish and a therapist who would "help" them on their way. It was not easy. It felt to me as if the people in the management team of the company we were working with did not want me there. The first five days were tough for me. However, the result was good. Kjell convinced me that it would feel better the very next time. He convinced me that this was something completely new and unknown to them. I understood but inside me there was a pain around it all. I flew home via Oslo. Slept there overnight to take the morning flight home to Stockholm again. Then I could check in my bag at the SAS hotel and then walk in the morning sun towards Forneby airport.

On the way there I found a small footpath out onto some rocks and a patch of grass. I walked down as I had time. I sat down there to meditate. Tears came and emotions welled up inside me. Exclusion, failure, I shouldn't exist, no one wants what I can give. All my old programs came to the surface clearly, I could see it. But the emotions were strong. Tears were running down my cheeks. I asked for help, asked for support to see if I was on the right path. I felt lost. Then a butterfly came flying and danced around me in the faint beautiful sunlight. An opening happened inside me. I saw it, but one butterfly was not enough to make me turn back home in trust. Then some more butterflies came. After a while, there must have been over a hundred butterflies dancing around me. I don't know how things happen but I had arrived at exactly the right time for them all to be born and dance out into the sun. Divinity and bliss is what I experienced. For me it was a sign and a divine gift. I was on the right path. My tears continued to flow but they turned into tears of total gratitude, love and trust. The experience was so beautiful and powerful that after that day, I never experienced this unbelief again. When I have been a little in disbelief, there has always been a sign, a butterfly or feather. Always some sign from life and divinity. And I have quickly been able to turn home in love and trust again.

On this journey with the project in Tromso, the next few times during the year were amazing. My role was so lovingly received and everyone who was part of this management team more or less transformed their lives.

Living with what is transforms. We have no other choice. In my case, I have had to step out of my own way many times. But every time it happens, life and I are in an amazing harmony. I bow to life and the invisible embrace life is!

CONFIDENCE IN LIFE

*L*ife is constantly changing. We cannot fight it. We have been children and we will grow older. We have seasons no matter what we want or think. If we put seeds in the ground, we need trust and patience for it to germinate and grow at its own pace. We try to control and manipulate but it comes from fear. If we talk about having trust in life, we need two things. Awareness and a loving, humble attitude.

We are not in control, life is bigger than that. What we can do is find confidence in the potential we have within us. Then embrace it.

The river of life is moving. But if we can be in the present and allow and trust what is here and now, we find a life in harmony. Allow your life potential, your life energy, the energy that is everything and the love within us. Let your whole being begin to live and come alive. As it was when we were children and the game just happened by itself. Let it start happening here and now. Let your inner self be your guide. When we can see the polarities and let them be there without choosing, a life of wholeness begins. A life of witnessing begins to happen. You are and you see and you can let all aspects of life be there without having to stop, without choosing anything. Your life becomes a dance where life happens and you follow along. To be able to see and to be without stopping.

We are the whole, but to understand and see more clearly, the wheel of life is there to help.

You can have faith in life. It is here for you.

When we don't trust ourselves or life, we often put the responsibility on others. We blame and we make ourselves irresponsible. It becomes the fault of others that things are not as you want them to be. The truth is that all possibilities live within you and you can change the situation. With trust, you can do it. The power and energy are then there for you. Or maybe it's not your job to change. Or maybe you can't. Life is bigger than both you and me. Then we must humbly and with trust in life relate to it. Trust that everything will happen as it should.

Our problem and our pain is that we constantly want something other than what is.

We want life, ourselves, our children, our partner to be something other than what they are. That we have a body that tells us off, that we ourselves, our children, are not well, that our partner struggles with expenses, tasks and emotions. We don't want to see what is here and now. We constantly want something else that we think is «better» for us than what is. In order to change direction and achieve something "better", we first need to stop and see what is. Not until we accept and face what is here and now with the emotions and depth it can mean, a change and transformation can take place. Not by running away and avoiding, but by stopping, seeing and accepting. Then change happens. Always to more space and love. That change happens as if by itself and that change transforms your life. It lasts forever.

FROM LEARNED KNOWLEDGE TO INNER WISDOM. THAT WISDOM IS YOURS TO FIND.

*O*ften, when we talk about knowledge, we are talking about learned knowledge.

When we turn our gaze home and into ourselves, truths and experiences on other levels than those learned. We then encounter the inner wisdom, life potential and loving richness that lives within us all.

But in order to discover it, we first need to see what is standing in our way

We have thoughts, we need to see and be clear about them. To start questioning whether they are ours and whether they are helpful and true for us at the moment. Thoughts can be difficult to see. But if we feel a sense of sadness, anger or discomfort and we stop and investigate, we may find a thought lying there, haunting us. Thoughts we don't see can be like a grain of sand in our eye. It hurts and we can't see why.

When we start to see and understand the thoughts and our mind, it is often a great relief but it can also feel scary as we often do not trust ourselves beyond them. Who are we then?

Who we are beyond thoughts and identity.

When we see how feelings and thoughts are connected, we can begin to dare to feel and understand ourselves on a deeper level.

When we begin to feel and see our thoughts and we no longer have a fight against but begin to want to understand and see, we go with life and an acceptance begins to happen. Acceptance is love and it heals us. It is the beginning of a wisdom that continues throughout life. A wisdom beyond the learned. A wisdom born of silence, a wisdom that is intuitive and that we can begin to see is in harmony with life itself.

Our spiritual heart is and will always be whole. To be able to see that is a tremendous liberation. We may have experienced painful events, hiding behind survival thoughts that keep us afloat in life. But when we see that within and beyond that, no harm has been done. You find yourself both transformed and whole.

Then there are unique qualities within you that yearn to live. Life wanted you here. Confidence in yourself and life.

Many people have asked me during my life if it is not hard to face people's emotions and all the stories we have. It certainly is not. We carry trapped emotional memories that lie within us as trapped life potential. Releasing and turning unconsciousness into loving understanding and presence is one of the most beautiful things I know. I know that it is only love. That we have not been allowed to live our potential for various reasons, not believed that we can be who we are or that mom could not love me and then become angry, sad and disappointed. When this is allowed to come to the surface and be released, we come to a feeling of just being love, the child within us is allowed to come home again and be who it is. The liberation is within us. It usually doesn't take many minutes when we turn our gaze home and consciously meet ourselves, no matter on what level, transformation takes place. Just the fact that we understand is important. I can't understand how we as sentient beings don't have more knowledge and courage to learn about what emotions are. That it is energy. Trapped emotions often have negative thoughts. Negative thoughts lead to negative behaviour. Towards ourselves and others. When we stop, meet, understand and can embrace what is with awareness, then transformation occurs. It leads to our negative thoughts being replaced with healthy energy and healthy behaviour. We are then in touch with a more loving energy and intelligence within us. By stopping and becoming aware, we can see that we are on the right path.

The intelligence of love. When we open the door of the heart, two things happen. The first is that what we previously locked up comes to the surface. Old pain needs to be released and reconciled. Then comes the unconditional love that is our true nature. The unconditional love that lives in all of us is healing and transforming. When not thoughts, old emotional memories and ideas from outside are in the way. To dare to forgive, reconcile and come to terms with what has happened in our history. To dare to live from the heart and the unconditional energy that lives there. That love is to live from wholeness. It is our true nature. This intelligence is about our heart being our inner transformer. Anything we think, feel or experience that we take to our heart is transformed. Take your thoughts to your heart and see what happens then. Meet your feelings in your heart and see what happens then. That presence knows. That presence has its own intelligence. Investigate and create your own experiences. That is when trust and the wisdom that lives in the conscious presence expands.

When we get in touch with our spiritual heart and it opens up, the emotions and memories that we previously locked up, come to the surface. Which is extremely important for us to get free energy flow again. What comes up we need to accept, feel and reconcile with. When we do that, our true life potential comes out.

All that we have locked up inside us lies like a lid over the authentically loving and creative longing that is our true life potential. So the therapeutic part of reconciling our history is for us to access the energy that is our truer flow. We can then live with the energy flow and what wants to happen as opposed to giving energy to fight against to keep down and keep away old memories. Which can lead to illness, bad relationships and burnout etc.

When we release energy by clearing our old emotional memories, a creativity, an inner longing and potential comes to life. A creativity and energy that is unique to you. Allowing and affirming your own life energy has its own intelligence. It is only by living it that we can see and expand in trust. When we do, it usually becomes clear how perfect life is. How pieces of the puzzle fall into place by themselves. But we need to take our steps and do what we are supposed to. Live ourselves, allow the energy that is you to be expressed. Whatever that looks like.

Creativity for me is not just painting a picture or dancing. Creativity is living. To clean when it needs to be done, to allow life to be lived in a true and healthy way. In these intense times, focusing one day at a time can be enough.

The intelligence of life energy itself. The one we can affirm and follow.

The more we get used to stopping and looking home, the more we understand the wholeness that lives within us. The more we can see the thoughts without getting stuck in them, without clinging and believing in them. The more we can allow sensations and emotions to become clear. The more unconditional presence we experience. The more we can allow ourselves to affirm the energy as it harmoniously and creatively wants. The more we can begin to see how life happens by itself. We can witness the events of life. We do not get stuck but see and flow lovingly along.

Trust in life and yourself is one. There is total unity and harmony.

In that presence and in that trust there is only peace and stillness.

A presence filled with wisdom. A presence and emptiness that we cannot see but experience and feel. An awareness where only trust and presence exist. To be one with the unlimited. From here all your decisions come.

This inner intelligence and wisdom guides us. It is in tune with the whole and lives in all of us.

But in order to grow high in our potential, we need to have roots within ourselves. Your wings are yours to fly with, but your roots need to grow.

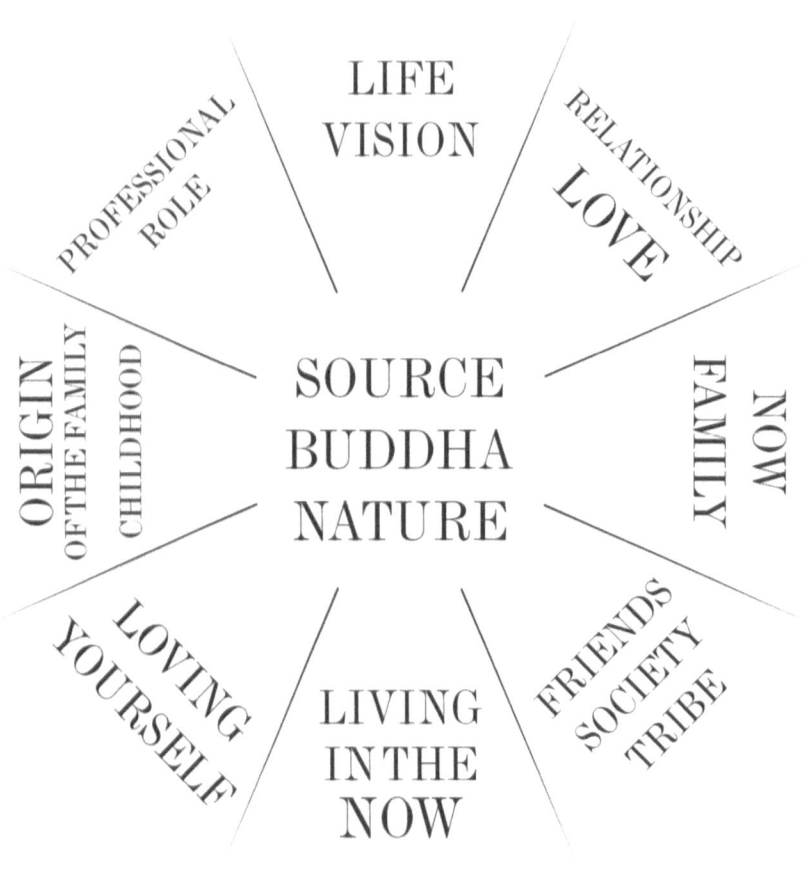

A drawn Wheel of Life

Premleena's Wheel of Life.

The art of seeing the bigger picture and transforming your own life.

General

With the Wheel of Life, I want to give you an opportunity to see your life in a larger perspective. To be able to understand where things belong and be able to sort them out. Just like we have it at home. We have our things in different rooms, not all in one big pile on the floor. That's how I felt I had it inside me before I started my inner journey. All the events and emotional memories were just packed in one big pile on top of each other.

With the Wheel of Life, I hope you will be able to see more clearly and increase your awareness so that you can dare to live yourself and your energy lovingly.

With awareness, you can find your inner source of wisdom and knowing. To befriend the love within you, what is true and a dignity to yourself and your life.

The base of my wheel of life

We all come from the whole. We are all the whole where nothing is missing us.

This whole has all polarities in it. When we allow ourselves to live in natural flow and harmony, all polarities can be present without getting stuck. Balance prevails.

We are each born as a unique individual with our own unique life path. We have everything and are perfect as we are.

But when we are born, we are born into a context that has been going on for a while. Our parents and their story. It is as if we are born into a theatre where a drama is taking place. We are shaped by that drama. We are not that story, but without awareness we often remain there, playing the role again and again.

In order to find our true life energy and path again, we need to understand what this history or family of origin has done to us. This understanding comes by stopping and bringing home our own feelings, seeing what thoughts and concepts we have trapped ourselves with.

When we are aware, we can free ourselves and find our inner longing and true nature. This process may take a lifetime but with the awareness of who you are beyond history, it doesn't matter. It will take time.

We all want to share our energy and have a good professional life. To find passion and joy in what we do. To give what we are here to give.

To find love in life. A love that is based on being able to give and melt with someone else. For that to happen, we need to like ourselves. Then we can take in and give from the inside out. The other becomes an opportunity to grow with, not an excuse to avoid looking at oneself.

Then, when we have children, if we choose to, the children can be children and we can act like adults.

Friends, society and the world are an extension of us. We are all one.

Learning to live and see in the present where I am. To accept and choose the situation I find myself in. Not fighting against but living with what is.
　　To dare to be here fully. To be able to love what is.

To feel your inner longing and dare to start affirming it. Find how you want to live your life, step by step in a direction that you feel is true for you.

To be able to see all the different parts, roles and aspects we have in life. To find passion, love and understanding for all the different parts and for your whole life. When we see and become aware, we can create balance and harmony. When we see more clearly, we can also relate with more presence.

I also want us to be able to see that our lives are not separate from the whole or life itself. We are part of a great infinite mystery. Where our life is unique and a gift to each of us. There is only one who can live your life truly and lovingly. That person is you. It is only you who knows your truths and your longings. These are answers you can find within you, nowhere else. Only you can understand, reconcile, listen and affirm your life.

I also want to convey with my wheel of life that we are energy and that through the wheel of life we can begin to feel confidence and be able to relate and become aware within us. From thought to feeling and beyond. To be able to live present and loving in trust and joy.

All the different parts have a natural connection and energy between them. All parts flow naturally and create a perfect balance. Seeing the wheel of life as a map and tool to help us understand where we are and where we long to go. How our history has affected us. That we can change. To be able to find loving, creative true paths for you. That you are the one who can take charge of your life. Only you know what you feel, what thoughts stand in your way. What longing lives inside you and what your truths look like.

It is only within you that that place exists that knows. To be able to discern from there a true yes.

The Wheel of Life has nine different parts. And all of them are important to understand and take in. They all interact with each other.

The fact that we can step into the roles we are supposed to step into also means that we can step out.

To see that we can rest within ourselves in the place that is still, quiet and whole. The part that is one with the whole. By seeing and understanding, we can make conscious choices. We can begin to own the right to our own lives.

To find your own natural inner energy. A human right, if you ask me.

To feel good about your own life. To be able to relax and flow with it. To be able to tackle what stands in your way. Invite yourself into your own life.

In the middle of the wheel of life is a quiet place, awareness.

The center that is in all of us. The inner peace and empty space that lives and is in harmony with the whole. The place where everything has its origin. Our inner source and buddha nature. The place that is just without thoughts and feelings. In this place we can rest and just be. This being fills our batteries. This space is the place that contains everything. It is not constant but an energy that expands and just is, in resonance with the whole.

Around this inner place are all the different aspects of life that have their opposites.

The wheel and life are moving.

The waves of energy go in and the waves of energy go out.

Living with the natural flow and movement of waves and energy.

(The nine different aspects

The present - Life vision and longing

Self-love and self-respect - Love relationship

The family of origin and our history - The Nu family

Job share with personal responsibility - Friends, community and world, a bigger we.

Our inner source and still buddha nature, the place that always has and always will be.)

Samsara is Sanskrit for wheel of life, a wheel that shows all the different aspects of life. A wheel of life that reflects or shows the drama of life. If we yearn for a change, it is in our inner being that the change has its beginning. We need to see the thoughts and feelings we have right now, if they match the life we long to live. If they are not, we have the opportunity to change it by becoming aware, to be able to step out of the way of ourselves.

What am I thinking? What do I feel? How do I live here now that it rules my life?

What if I explore truer thoughts for myself here and now, how do I feel then? What kind of life am I living if I shift my focus? It doesn't matter what I think, the point is whether I believe what I think or not. When I believe the thought, it is like a grain of sand in my eye and it blinds me. When I have distance to the thought, I can see. Then the grain of sand is out of my eye and I can realize that it was just a grain of sand. The colour then does not matter so much.

Many years ago I saw Buddhist monks creating samsara wheels of life in coloured sand. It was on one of my trips to India. They stood in meditation, mindfulness, for a whole day creating different wheels of life in beautiful different coloured sand. When it was finished, one of the monks took his hand and pulled it straight across. Everything disappeared. The transience of life. We are alive. We give what we have to give. When it is done, it is done. Everything has a beginning, a middle and an end.

This made an extremely strong impression on me.

The wheels of life were so beautiful and had the most amazing patterns. Everyone was different. Everyone was in balance.

Here you will create and be able to see your wheel of life, your Samsara. When we see what it looks like right now, we can see what we want to change and how we want to live.

By using my Wheel of Life, you can raise your awareness and see the big picture more clearly. Where you are right now. What longings you have. You can see your different roles, how you are controlled by old ideas and thought patterns. You can also start to rest in and see your innermost quiet space. Rest in what is quiet, still and present all the time around you and in you.

When we live in harmony with what is, expansion happens naturally. Life wants us to grow and expand. Life constantly wants the best for us. And it is only by living and exploring that it can become your truth.

Change happens and everything moves. Being able to see that everything is happening as it should and that events have a coherence, an interplay.

Learning to live with life and yourself.

My wheel of life has nine different parts of life, one of which is a center in the middle that we can call our inner still place, our inner source or our inner buddha nature. The place within us that is pure energy. Being empty beyond the thoughts of who we should be or are.

Without the ideas we have about ourselves. To just be able to be. The quality we all come from. Here it is still and filled with a presence vibrating with the whole universe.

All eight parts complement each other and each part has its counterforce.

No part is more important than the other. All are included. And all are necessary. And all are preconditions for each other. It is also the case that the different parts are activated at different times in our lives. A job situation may be relevant. Or a love relationship activates the whole wheel of life.

Having a living wheel of life that you are aware of is a great gift to yourself. To be able to see more clearly how all nine parts interact with each other and set the whole wheel of life in motion.

They are all part of the samsara of life, the drama and events of life.

When we can look at our life from a wider perspective, it becomes easier to understand and relate. It becomes clearer to see when we have an overview. It is also the case that if we can see, we can step in and act more clearly and we can also step out and just let ourselves be.

An open mind. Letting go of old thoughts and ideas. Just like a computer needs updating, we need to update our old thinking about ourselves and life.

A warm heart where old feelings can come to the surface and no longer be trapped. To let our sensitivities, our senses and our longings come to life.

A living soul where our inner self can be expressed. Present and alive.

What am I thinking?
What does the opposite look like?
What do I feel? What is my truth?
How do I live when I think and feel like that?
How would I live then?

What if I let my inner self guide me?
Which feels truest and or most loving?
What are my choices?
What do I give my energy to? Grief and old identity or to more awareness and love?

Drew a circle with a yin / yang symbol in the middle and the nine
   Yin and yang, or your inner buddha nature with all eight parts around…like a cake.

A flower is not its shell. The potential of the flower itself lives in the seed. The same is true of us. We are not our shell. We are the energy that lives within us. To stop and look inward, to see and understand beyond the shell is to transform and open up to the greatness of life, potential and the mystery of who we are. To be able to shift focus from separation and pain to a life of wholeness, love and harmony. To go from being identified with the shell to start allowing oneself to live with oneself and the path of life potential. We don't need to become anything, we already are. All that needs to happen is for us to step out of the way of ourselves so that the flowering can happen.

In each aspect see what you are thinking, feel what energy and emotions are there.
   What longing is inside you?

"Without your story,
you are perfectly fine"

BYRON KATIE

1. LIVING IN THE NOW.

You have never been anywhere else but here and now. The present is perfect, just as it is. This is where all the energy is. Nowhere else. Stop and take in this now without a fight on any level. Everything you've done and been through has led you to this very moment. Take it in. You should not be anywhere else but here. All energy and wisdom is here. Love the present totally and fully just as it is.

It is totally open and embraced. When we stop here and now, we see that not a single real problem prevails. The problems are only in our minds which are not blinding us from seeing the present.

Learning to listen and breathe in each new moment....

Life is what is happening right NOW! Everything is already there. Choose what is now... Stop and take it in. It's just a matter of understanding and listening to the wisdom that is here. In the present is the power that takes you forward and to the next now. Your longing. That power lives here in the present. Find your focus, find your intention. One of the first steps is to be able to live anchored in the present. Take your life seriously. Not boring or heavy, but with the realization that there is only one of you and there is only now and there is only you who knows your path.

General

We have never been anywhere else but in the present. This is where all the energy is.

If we live in constant struggle that things should be different in the here and now, we cannot feel happiness and contentment. It comes the moment we openly choose to see and be in what is here and now. No matter how it is. If we long for change, the first step needs to be full acceptance of the situation first. Everything we have been through has led you up to this moment. Life is perfect and we constantly get what we need. What makes the journey of life feel more glorious is that we are here in this moment, consciously taking in how life is vibrating in and around us perfectly as it should.

Living from presence and awareness in the present is one of the greatest gifts we can give to ourselves.

Everything we have been through has brought us to this moment. When we live in the present, we discover that there are no problems here. Our problems, worries and pain are based on the past and what we think the future will bring. In the present we are free and in a relaxed present there is no fear. Fear means believing our thoughts about what the future will bring. Learning to live in the present, resting and trusting the present.

We often find it difficult to live in the present. We either dream ourselves away or live in the past, i.e. our thoughts are usually elsewhere. Thoughts separate us from really seeing and being where we are.

Thoughts blind us. Trust and living in the moment go hand in hand.

If we don't trust, it's hard to rest in the present. Then we want to get out of here quickly. Or just remember how it used to be. We let our focus go to the past or dream about the future.

Since the source of energy is only in the present, there will be no energy if we let our thoughts rule. We will get nowhere.

In the present moment there is also an intuitive wisdom and a presence that allows us to act and respond in a present way.

Things don't always turn out the way you expect them to, but they do!

The body is the bearer of our entire history. It makes it clear here and now.

When we can step out of all our ideas and just be in the moment, we can experience peace, relaxation and feel the intuitive power and wisdom that is there.

About myself.

When I lived my life unaware of who I was. My life was empty, I had no confidence. And every now was just a repetition.

When I stopped, turned my gaze inward and thus began to clear up my history, I landed in the present completely empty. I could see. I could feel.

The experience of being the vibrant energy that just is, is perfection. There and then, trust came into my life. And I have followed that intuitive feeling ever since. That was almost thirty years ago and from the depths of myself I wish to convey that LIFE and NOW CARRY US. It works. And if it does for me, it does for you. To go with life and not against. Life, the present and your life energy are the same.

The challenges are there. Right now for me it is putting my journey into words and writing.

Where I try to put into words the gift of living in trust. It starts with stopping and understanding your life. Start here and now. It is the greatest gift you can give yourself. And it is a perishable commodity. I stepped out of the way of myself and landed in the infinite presence of now.

Life changes and we expand. With trust, we can let life happen in its natural form. I have trusted my inner intuitive feeling and I follow it. It has carried me so beautifully into the next now with new amazing gifts. It has been and is a wonderfully exciting and loving journey. I could never have imagined or planned all the gifts that have come to me. I have accepted them, doing my utmost from my own truth.

If I have felt discouraged, I have asked for a sign. Right now, no confidence. Then life has given me signs. It may sound strange when I write this. But the truth is that hundreds of butterflies have surrounded me. Feathers have fallen and settled at my feet and from feeling nothing one moment to feeling a presence that has just embraced me the next.

Many tears have run down my cheeks and the tears have again and again cleared away the old. And opened my heart in trust and presence. Again and again.

The confidence that comes when we are and can receive the present. The confidence that grows stronger when we see that our steps, one by one, carry us. Confidence is in your hands.

I have followed life. It is a great gift to live like that.

There has never been money as a security for me. My energy and trust in my inner self have been and are the wealth I feel. And that life gives us what we need.

Not having collateral in the bank has meant that I have had to act and share and be true to myself. I have never been able to "cheat" or be lazy.

Which is a good feeling. To do what I am supposed to do.

And rest in it, ride along.

In the present lies the power that takes us forward in life.

Today, the present is my source and truest friend.

Client example

A man, Erik, 35, came to me. His girlfriend had sent him.

He found it hard to see his own weaknesses. But life had brought him to a situation he found hard to handle. He had lots of dreams and visions for himself and his surroundings. But rarely, if ever, did any of his ideas come to fruition. He could speak for himself, so both his girlfriend and his bosses believed strongly in his capabilities. By now, both his girlfriend and his bosses were getting fed up. That's where I come in.

We look at the Wheel of Life and see that his life visions are entirely possible.

The road there starts first with landing in the present.

See what it looks like right now.

The energy is in the present.

In the present there are also the emotions. Impatience, fear. Sadness.

Everything came to the surface for my client.

He had fought against this.

But when we started to see clearly what it was, he realized that it was emotions and that he could handle them.

Fighting back can take a lifetime. Becoming aware that we have feelings, accepting them, seeing them. Feeling them takes a few minutes.

When my client began to rest in himself on a deeper level, he discovered much more relaxation and the impatience disappeared. He saw that his visions were good. And he was able to put a structure on how he could start listening and stop and be in the moment.

This is where the energy and insights were. Not "over there".

His girlfriend was lovingly initiated into his life here and now. With a clear loving goal. She supported him and she understood.

His bosses also started to understand. He had to attend a leadership course with me to learn how to live here and now. He needed to work on finding a direction and seeing how he could manage and manifest what he wanted. It's going from dreaming to living and realizing. One step at a time.

A client of mine, Arne, a man of forty-five years. Married with two children aged between ten and twelve.

He was a businessman with a seemingly good life. His job situation meant that he had to travel and fly a lot. The flights were many and sometimes quite long.

He needed help to manage his fear of flying, which had not gotten easier but was getting stronger and harder for him to manage. It was getting worse and stronger every time.

When he came to me, he was in dire need of sorting out the problem.

We started looking at how he was living now. Everything was fine as he saw it. His relationship with his wife and his role as a father to their two children. Although he had some guilt about not being at home and being able to share all the everyday life.

We went over what his childhood had been like. His childhood was relatively normal. There was nothing big or dramatic.

Like most of us, he had luggage with him. But it was not a major problem. He couldn't understand why he was having panic attacks with difficulty breathing and chest tightness before flights.

When we started talking about living in the moment. his whole face lit up.

He said he found it difficult to live in the present. He was always going somewhere in his mind.

He lived ten thoughts ahead, he said.

What was the reason? What was the reason?

We got back to his childhood.

Of course, the man realized that he had to shut down his emotions early on. Become a good boy. Just like his father. He had decided early on that he would never be like his father. He had worked on that when it came to his own children. He had gotten to know them, supported them and been there for them much, much more than his father ever could have been.

But the feelings he had locked up early on had largely remained inside him.

When he was not in control of his emotions in certain situations, he panicked.

We started there and then a training in starting to feel.

He started practicing stopping and taking in the present.

With his wife. With his children and in his professional life.

His biggest challenge was when he had to fly.

With all the fears that he could not control at the time.

There his emotional life had come to the surface.

He could see that since he was a child he had had to control his emotions.

His father had sternly told him at an early age that he and boys should not cry. Therefore, by nature, he had cried very little in his life.

He could see and he understood that this flying was associated with his father. All these air captains with their power.

It becomes and is so incredibly interesting when we start to see the bigger picture of us. How things, people and events are connected.

Sometimes I feel like the Sherlock Holmes of the soul, a real detective work to find the inner keys. They are there. You just have to look a little.

Most of us try to control our emotions.

If we understand that they are part of our human nature, if we learn to be with them in the present. Let them have their place, they will come and go quite quickly.

That was the experience for my client.

Before getting on the plane. This time he could stay sober and not take pills. His mind was spinning a hundred and eighty. It's not going to work. I'm going to die. I'm going home again. Premleena is crazy to put me through this etc. We were in touch by phone so he could see that it was his thoughts that were haunting him as he sat there in the waiting room. He felt that he was insecure when feelings came up inside him. He had learned early in his life to control them.

Then, as he walked up the stairs into the plane, a warmth spread through him. He accepted the situation. He breathed slowly and deliberately. He was in the moment. One moment at a time.

The journey went well. His thoughts had tried to scare him several times. But his intention with himself was to breathe and to be in the moment with himself. To not let the thoughts take away his presence.

This trip was a major turning point for this man.

He also began to embrace more of his emotional life. His thoughts had ruled far too much.

Thanks to this situation, and this panic about flying, something happened. That he could not have any control. That panic made him aware and he was able to expand and embrace himself and get to know the feelings that he was carrying. They are not dangerous, they just need to come to the surface. They gave him a deeper understanding of himself.

His wife and children also began to feel more seen and the whole family became a more vibrant and loving family.

Exercise

Life is what happens here and now.

Stop and take in your now.
Close your eyes for a moment. Become aware that your body is breathing. Help a little and increase the intake of air, when you exhale, relax a little extraLet your body find a more relaxed position.
When you've settled down a bit here and now.
Feel how it feels on the inside of yourself.
Breathe calmly.
Allow air to enter the whole body.
Let the breath go away.
Relax a little deeper.
Ask your body what it is feeling.
What thoughts are there.
Just look and become aware.
Completely without judgment. Nothing needs to be done.
See for yourself.
Just let yourself rest in yourself and see.
Maybe a tear will come.
Let it come, it is the heart that relaxes.

Write down when you opened your eyes again:
What life cycle are you living in today?

....

....

....

....

Is there anything that "grates" in your life?
What thoughts and/or feelings are you aware of?

....

....

....

What touches your heart and brings joy and energy to your life?

....

....

....

Can you rest and relax in the present? What wisdom is here for you?

....

....

....

How can you practice being fully present in the moment?

....

....

....

Let all aspects of the wheel of life be experienced and illuminated in the present and let all aspects come alive with its longing and inner potential that lives in every part.

2. LOVE YOURSELF AND YOUR HUMAN NATURE

*Y*ou are the friend you have been waiting for. You are perfect and you are unique. Your inner longings are here for you to realize them. Your life is yours and it happens within you, nowhere else.

The most important thing of all. You were perfect when you were born. Your open innocent being was in total harmony. Everyone has their unique path, tone and energy. It's just a matter of listening and being able to embrace it. As you begin to know yourself, a feeling of love will come.

Everything starts and ends with you.

No relationship is better or worse than the one you have with yourself.

Finding trust and love for yourself is one of the prerequisites for living in harmony. To find your value.

Being able to relate to your body, your feelings, see your thoughts and learn to listen to your inner self. See your thoughts that stand in the way of living your potential.

General

The deeper the connection to yourself, the deeper the connection to others and life.

Each individual is love and each has a unique expression.

Get to know that individual. Beyond the thoughts.

Your love relationships reflect parts that you have with yourself.

Learning to accept, respect and love yourself.

The body is the house you live in.

The first is to learn to listen and relate to our bodies. The body is a carrier, like a house, of all that you carry. It is not that the body, the thoughts, the feelings and our inner nature are separate from each other. Everything is connected. If we put down a lot of emotional memories, the body will carry them. If we have negative thoughts, it's as if we're beating ourselves up all the time.

If we don't listen to the quiet still inner nature that lives within us. Then we close that door on ourselves. The door to the place where we can rest and replenish our batteries, the place that has a wisdom beyond the intellect. The place that is in tune with the whole and the entire universe.

If your body and you can be compared to a house with different rooms. The wheel of life is an opportunity to go inside ourselves and clean up our inner rooms. The room where the love for yourself lives. What does it look like there?

Just as every flower is unique, so are you.

The life potential that lives in you and is on a truer plane, you can only learn to listen to, expand in and allow yourself to be trusted.

Just like a seed. Finding the unique life energy that lives in you.

We've all heard the old adage that it's important to love and care for yourself.

Here it comes again.

All relationships start and end with you. If you like you, it reflected in the relationship. If you don't like you, it is reflected in the relationship.

Liking yourself is not an ego boost. It means you start to understand who you are and who you are not. Of course, it's different depending on what age you are. What stage of life you are in. What gender you are. But the deeper you connect with yourself, the deeper your understanding of yourself can be. You can feel the trust and love that comes with accepting and listening to yourself. To get to know yourself as the unique person you are, is to dare to trust and have a yes to getting to know yourself.

Being able to step out of the way of yourself and the life potential that lives there.

You naturally want to be able to feel an unconditional love for yourself.

Of course, you also want to know what you long for. What your needs are. And who you are right now. Find confidence in yourself.

It is difficult to have a good relationship with others if I do not know who I am.

What your needs are. Can you listen to yourself and your body, the house you live in? How does it feel?

Today, we are so fixated on our bodies alone that we have often forgotten that they even have feelings. The result is that we run over ourselves. It can be too painful to stop in the here and now as the old emotional memories lie there under the surface and want to surface.

It makes us run away from ourselves instead of stopping, to start seeing, start feeling and start understanding. To stop running away from ourselves. And instead stop and understand ourselves more deeply. That journey can start now. The body is the house we live in.

The thoughts, are they yours or have you inherited them? The feelings, are you aware of the truth behind them?

Your unique expression, what is it? And the quiet still voice of your soul, do you listen to it and rest in trust in the presence and wisdom that prevails here?

The body is like an innocent child. The body is amazing with all that it creates for us. So we can live. It just receives and it just gives unconditionally. We need to learn to listen.

The body wants to communicate. It is the carrier of all emotional memories, all feelings and all energy from day one of our lives until now.

The body has its own energy system.

Seven different energy levels of energy live in our bodies. This is where the life energy meets the body. We cannot see the different energy levels but we can feel them.

The body's energy levels

- The base. Colour red. It is our survival and security living here. It stands for the material. The sexual. When we do not feel confidence here, the body can respond with constipation, problems in our abdomens. If we don't have confidence in our power to survive, we compensate on the outside by acquiring material things and bank accounts where money is not in a flow.

- Second energy space, a little below the navel and behind the tail. Orange color. This is where our vulnerability and emotions live. This is where we take in energy. This is where shocks get stuck in the system. So if we are carrying shocks, we can put our hands here. Close our eyes and feel how we can breathe softly here. Breathe out and relax. Allow tears or just let a deep relaxation happen. Our inner little child lives here. When we process our emotional memories, the door to our senses opens and they come alive.

- Third is our power center. Yellow color. This is where our power lives. It can be seen as a sun. Shining.

  Often we have not been allowed to affirm this power, but our inner critics and judges sit here and belittle.

  One technique that I generally recommend is The Work by Byron Katie. That technique of looking at your thoughts is extremely valuable here at this level. In our world where competition to be better than or worse than is allowed to rule our lives. Something we learned early on. Step out of the way and all of us can shine like suns. All our opposites and opposites need to be included.

- Fourth is our heart and body transformer. Green or pink color. Here the unconditional love lives in us. Innocent energy. It is the place in us that can embrace everything. Here all energy meets. Our masculinity meets our femininity. Our darkness meets the light. The roots down into ourselves meet the sky. The energy of the heart is like nature, healing and non-judgmental. The quality that lives in our hearts has the ability to transform and heal all the different parts within us.

- Fifth is our creative and communicative center. Sitting in the throat and back of the neck. To create and communicate what is true for us. Listening and feeling ourselves and letting our unique energy be expressed.

- Sixth is the level where intuition lives. Third eye. To know without having read in a book. The place of wisdom. A mind that is open beyond thought. An intelligence beyond the learned.

- Seventh is the top, the crown of our heads. The opening up to the universe where multiple levels of energy centers exist. It is the fontanel of small children who are completely soft and open when we are born. Open as we are one with the whole. It is physically soft so that we can be born and come out. It grows again and when we are about six months old that gate has closed again. But with awareness and presence, we can feel how that opening can become alive again.

When all these energy levels are allowed to be alive and open, our life becomes rich. It is like an instrument with many notes. A flute with seven different notes that life can play. Or like a color map where all the colors can be used.

In my own case.

As I described earlier, my mother was a great challenge for me growing up. In my childhood, when she still lived at home, she started dieting every Monday. She, who in my eyes was extremely beautiful, constantly complained about how she looked. She was too fat and there was a constant feeling that she was not ok. She was constantly wearing beautiful clothes but it wasn't enough. She gave me a picture of what she thought I should look like. A picture of a model, tall and thin. I, who had been small and short all my life, got strong ideas about how wrong I was. I got breasts and round shapes, not good in my world. I barely ate and tried to become thin and tall. It didn't work out well. An attempt to become a model came when I was sixteen. But I was too shy to even open up to the photographer. The pictures were published in the women's world, but I don't think my mother even saw them.

I was just trying to survive. I didn't want to be with me. I found it extremely difficult to see myself.

I had nightmares at night. I was not feeling well. I didn't like myself at all.

My thoughts about myself were negative and weighed me down. With those thoughts that were critical and judgmental, it was impossible to love myself. I just stuffed my feelings inside myself, unconsciously. I went on thinking that everything was wrong with me. In that pain-filled and unconscious state, I was guided by being right. I.e. I believed that I am not worthy of being loved. I lived as if that was the truth.

Today, I can understand how that identity put a lid on everything else. It "gave" me the right not to like myself. That thought gave me a mandate that I didn't fit in. I was wrong.

I don't think there is a single person who would think there was a problem with my height. The thought that was constantly spinning in my head was "I'm too short". That thought was like a lid over my whole being. All the pain that lay underneath I couldn't handle. I didn't even know it was there.

The day I opened the lid and got in touch with me all the way home in my own heart. That's when everything turned around.

I realized that I was not my thoughts. I realized that I am not my feelings either. I began to feel a love behind all that I had previously identified with. I felt vibrant life energy. It was just there. Nothing that I put there. It was life itself vibrating within me. There was a stillness and peace within me that I could rest in. Life and I are not and were not separated into two parts, we were one. We are and have never been in any contradiction. We are and have always been ONE energy. I love who I am from the inside out. I love you and I love me.

Today, the relationship with myself and the love I experience is the basis for all my other relationships.

So the question searchers have been asking themselves for thousands of years is "who am I?"

Something I came to understand during my years with Osho. I had been so unaware that people were searching for the truth about themselves for thousands of years. One thing is certain. We are not our thoughts. They come and go. We have not created our thoughts. Feelings have never been a problem. But they become so when we lock them up. Thoughts come and go. Feelings come and go. We are like the open sky where everything happens and everything comes and goes. However, the sky is always here.

Who are we where it comes and goes? Our true nature is the one who sees. The presence.

Client example

One of the most common reasons for starting to look at oneself is that relationships are not working so well. When couples contact me and want to come to have a working relationship, I always work with the individual. No relationship is better than the relationship you have with yourself. In all sessions and in all courses I have given, it is about increasing your own awareness and understanding. I meet many people who doubt that there will be a change on the outside when we "only" work with ourselves. I remember one participant in particular, Anita, who came to stop for a while. She was almost a workaholic. She came because her temper and anger were destroying her. She was capable, sometimes too fast and capable for her own good.

Stopping and looking inward was not easy for this driven woman. When she arrived, she also told me that she might have to take calls. She had applied for a new job and might hear back in the next few days. As the days passed, she got to know her body and the energy that lived there. She was a daddy's girl and when she arrived, she had difficulty with her emotions. This was reflected in her relationship with her daughter, now 14. They had big strong fights at home. The daughter was also overweight, which bothered the woman who had extreme control over her weight. She wanted and tried to control most things. This control was slowly released and she started to get to know herself. She began to see what thoughts and ideas she had that blocked out all vulnerability, femininity and sensitivity. She got in touch with her inner child. The girl she once was had been locked up in goodness. This was to gain her father's love. She did not have much contact with her mother. A sister had arrived just over a year after she was born. Her self-image lay in being a good girl. She had never liked either her body or who she was. Now, during our days together, a sensitive, beautiful woman emerged. She felt more and more whole inside. As she said, "It was as if I had only lived the male part of me. Now I'm going home to be a loving mother. See the beauty of my daughter."

She did. Her daughter had felt seen for the first time. The woman began to like herself more and more. Her sensitivity was allowed her life. A few days after the course, she called to say that she had got the new job she had applied for, a top job. She had told the company she was going to work for that she was not quite the same as when she had applied for the job before. She was not less of herself but more. There had been parts of her that she had not been in touch with before. She loved herself now! They wanted her to start but as she said herself. It's important to bring these qualities into your work too. To love oneself is to understand oneself.

General

Get to know yourself from the inside. See all the thoughts you have about yourself that hold you back. Learn to listen to your body. See the different energy levels that live in you. Allow your body and life energy to come alive. Breathe, feel and affirm yourself.

Exercise

Stop - your inner self is waiting! An exercise in increasing love for yourself.

What does self-love mean to you, in depth?

....

....

....

What does it mean to fully respect yourself?

....

....

....

How do you feel about yourself? Your body, your emotions, your mind?

....

....

....

What events have you locked in your heart? Open your heart so you can feel it love that lives there.

....

....

....

What are you looking forward to?

....

....

....

Do you trust and listen to your inner voice?

....

....

....

How would you live if you loved yourself fully?

....

....

....

Do you allow yourself to be happy in life?

....

....

....

We all have a receptive side that receives and we all have an active side that gives and does.

Do you have a balance between your giving of energy and being able to receive?

What would you need to do to help you find balance?

....

....

....

Take a long walk or similar and talk it out with yourself. The way you would want your best friend to relate to you. Listen and feel yourself for a while. Let go of all focus on what is outside yourself. After that, write a love letter to yourself, how you want to live with you, how you want to get to know you, how you want to forgive you.

....

....

....

What unique qualities, strengths and talents do you feel you have?

....

....

....

Who are you here and now beyond all ideas about yourself?

....

....

....

Executive summary

You are your own unique individual with unique qualities and talents. Open up the life potential that lives in you. Seek all avenues to truly love yourself and your life.

Get to know that person! What thoughts and feelings you have.What your heart carries and longs for.What unique quality and creativity lives in you.Learn to rest in your inner self.

Let that person travel in confidence in the adventure of life without the heavy backpack.

Find the confidence and trust in her or him.

Raise your awareness. Deepen your connection with yourself.

Then your truths become clear to you. Then you can feel your inner intuitive feeling and let your inner wisdom come out. To trust it is to be able to relax into yourself.

Life is the river and you can learn to relax.

This can only happen if we understand.

Start exploring within yourself how you want to live and be with you through life.

Take care of your body, the house that you live in, but don't just stop at that but examine yourself in depth. From thought, to feeling, to your heart where acceptance and healing reside. Know your unique qualities and learn to rest in the present without ideas that it should be any other way. Draw strength from there. Rest in your inner quiet space and let it expand.

Understand how she/he has been feeling.

Creating a good relationship with ourselves means understanding who we are and what we are not.

Love you, you are unique and have a unique journey.

Only you know, only you can find out your truths.

The challenge

To dare to be alone. To dare to listen and follow your own inner voice. To take space and time with who you are. To be able to reconcile with yourself and your history. To be able to "bring home" the little child within us. To open up all the doors that were closed during childhood. To open your heart so that healing, wholeness and expansion can take place.

Byron Katie's technique 'The Work' is a fantastic tool to use to get beyond the thoughts and instead find your own truths. In order to love yourself fully, you need to understand yourself deeply. To understand yourself, you need to embrace your inner self and the history and identification you carry. This brings us to the next aspect of the Wheel of Life.

3. ORIGIN OF THE FAMILY
AND CHILDHOOD

*W*e cannot run away from our history. We can try to repress, but not escape. What we can do is start understanding the history you are born into. Here you were a child. The opportunity to get to know and understand you as a child again, from the inside. Not how you learned to be but how it was for you, understanding the child from within. Being able to see how this affects and guides you today. Understanding and starting to reconcile, accept, allows you to grow up beyond your story. You are not your story but understanding it and reconciling with it and your parents is extremely important for a full life. Otherwise, it lies dormant in all different parts of life. Find what is you and true beyond it.

We all have a history, but it does not have to control us. We have inherited parts of history, and you are the one who can make sure that this legacy stops, otherwise it will be passed on generation after generation. Your children will be the ones to take over. With awareness and insights, we can expand beyond it.

Your understanding and coming to terms with your history happens within you. It is about your experiences, and you can begin to understand and reconcile what you have previously had to shut down in order to survive. If we don't see what history has done to us, there is a risk that it will control us in the subconscious. We can get to know ourselves beyond it. So let yourself become aware of your history so you can free yourself and your life energy. Whatever has happened has happened.

The more you understand, the more distance, the freer you become. All children are whole and totally unique. But we often shut down that unique quality early on when we are born into a story that has been going on for a long time with a lot of repressed pain for a long, long time. Maybe you're the first in your family to stop and look inside yourself. You are the first in hundreds of years to experience that beyond all your learned programs and pains, you are whole.

The more you understand how you felt as a child, the more you reconcile with your parents and the history they carry. The better you can understand your own children. And the better you can take your parental role. History itself is not the problem. The problem is that we carry unprocessed memories and inherited thoughts that have come to rule our lives from our subconscious. The thoughts about who we are or are not have come between you and your inner self. The contact that once existed in you as a child has been lost. No one is at fault, everyone has done the best they could based on their level of awareness. Unconsciousness equals disconnection.

General

The early years of our childhood.

When we are born, it is as if we are born onto a theater stage. A stage that has its play. This play has been going on for a long time before you arrived. A play with different given roles. It became a role here. You were a child who was just pure life energy.

Our roles can be divided into three different categories.

As a triangle with a receptive part which we can call here the OFFER, a part which is the powerful part which we can call here the TYRANT and a part which is the HELPER.

Rectangular triangle
Power, vulnerability and helper

This triangle was created by a therapist named Karpman.

When we are children, we step into this 'Family Triangle'.

I myself stepped in and became a victim. My mother was the tyrant in that she wanted to leave and thus threatened the family and me. My father and my brothers were the helpers. The roles changed when my mother left the family. Dad then became the victim and I his helper.

When we don't see this, the role stays with us as we grow up. It's just that we fill the triangle with new people. This may become apparent in relationships and at work etc.

What we need to understand and bring home are all these roles and qualities. We are all powerful, we are all receptive and sensitive and we can all understand and help ourselves. When we own all the qualities, the energy starts to flow and it goes from being a game between individuals in a triangle to becoming a circle of wholeness and harmony.

Maybe you had siblings who already existed or who came later.

There were your parents, whether they were present or not, your grandparents. There were family ties in all different directions far back in time. You took the role that was yours to take. As a child, it was the most intelligent thing you could do at the time no matter what it was. As children, we were just energy and we were emotions. Until one day we locked up all the emotions and put labels on who you thought you were.

What you have then done is that you have grown up and forgotten and just continued to 'play' the same role. You have replaced mom and dad with a partner. Or work colleague. You continue to manifest the family image and your role in all different ways. As you become more aware, you may ask yourself whether you want to continue in the same way or whether you want to disengage.

As energy and whole people, we are all the qualities. The so-called tyrant energy means that we own our power and our direction. Helper means to begin to understand and help oneself. To be a victim is to acknowledge your quiet depth, vulnerability and emotional life. In that understanding, the energy can flow freely. In the triangle, the energy stops and you have to deal with actors in the different areas that you yourself do not own. In our childhood, you were a child with a lot of emotions. That child needs your attention so you can understand how you experienced life then. Healing, reconciliation and liberation can only happen in awareness and in our hearts. It cannot be understood with the intellect alone. The energy that lives in the heart transforms the energy like a butterfly transforms from a chrysalis. And you become aware that it is your story and that you have taken on a role.

Once we got into a role. Then we were a child. That child carries a unique life energy. That child needs somewhere to come home and be understood, how he or she has been. So that the energy there can be released. That energy is love.

You are the person who can start listening. Understand and get to know the "child" inside you.

It is extremely valuable to get to know ourselves and the history we carry.

What was my experience like?

Not how I think about them now.

Energy is stuck in old roles and ideas.

That's where the love and creativity, the power and the unique potential of life is.

You were once just free loving energy where everything was included.

We expressed ourselves through our feelings. Before the words came.

Until the day you understood.

Here's an example. You are a small child who has just been given a nice red plastic car to play with in the sandpit. Other children also come there. After a while, when you have been proudly playing with the car, another child comes and takes it from you. You as a child start screaming and crying "the car is mine". Your mother then steps in and says "little x give little y your car. You can have it later. Please let it go!" Mom gives the car to the other child. In your world, the following happens. Aha, mom is on his side. I'm just going to settle down and not fight, I was so excited about my new toy. I shut down my natural emotions and box them in. After all, I'm dependent on my mom and do what she says.

Mom says "don't be sad about it".

I feel sad. But I can't have these feelings. I try to shut down and because I'm not supposed to be like me, I have to be and behave like the others. My natural self is replaced by seeing how others are and that I should be like them.

This natural energy shuts down our natural way of being early on.

We then lose touch with ourselves. Our self-esteem disappears.

And all focus must go to looking at the outside.

Even if that has been the case, which it seems most of us have had in different ways, we can put it right now.

About me and my story

Growing up with my story, it is valuable to see and understand what my mom and dad carried. Why couldn't they be more loving and understanding. My mother grew up in an orphanage in northern Sweden. For three years she was there without being 'chosen' and without anyone caring. She eventually came to my grandfather and grandmother. I'm sure my grandfather was happy to have this little girl, but my grandmother was more hard-headed. Perhaps she was because of Grandpa's love for his daughter. Grandma obviously couldn't have children and was probably in pain about it.

My mother's wounds probably ran very deep in the subconscious. She never told me that she was adopted. She never processed this pain, which has rarely happened. But as children, we are like sponges and feel the pain that our parents invisibly carry. She left me with my father who was wounded by his history. My grandmother had died when my father was young. He was the oldest of four siblings. He had three younger sisters. He was born in in the south part of Sweden, poor and unreligious. When he was eighteen, he left home. All I know is that he wanted to get away and went to Norway. After a while he came back but never to his hometown. So when my mom leaves him, his pain comes to life. I think that pain made him afraid. I as a child unconsciously choose to be there emotionally for him. His needs became more important than mine. My older brothers were there too, but they were adults and on their way out in life.

Later in life, when I chose a spiritual path, my father went mad at me for a while. On the one hand, I think his old religious history is being brought up. On the other hand, I blame him for not being there emotionally for me. With awareness, there is no guilt on my part. Emotions I have needed to release within me. Anger, sadness and disappointment. But it has been necessary for me to get free energy within me, not as a blame.

My childhood patterns have been clearly reflected in my life. In all my relationships and in my professional life. I have sought both a mother and a father on an unconscious level.

When I project my father onto the world around me, I have become the helper who gives and gives and gives. I completely lose touch with my own needs. I become what they call codependent.

When I project mom on the outside, I often get love and closeness on one level only to have the person disappear without me perhaps understanding why. Psychopathic traits that some men in my life have had.

When I set my family straight in my mind through awareness and love, there is only more and more openness to life. I no longer need the reflections and challenges that came before.

The more loving I feel, the more loving life becomes.

The journey home into myself beyond who I thought I was. It became a beginning of a spiritual and whole journey that has just begun and has no end. When history is no longer the truth of who I am, I can only see how life is lived by itself and I lovingly follow along. I and we are totally loved and cared for all the time. Stay open and without any curtains of thought and you can feel that truth.

My inner nature was free and unspoiled. It was vibrant with loving life.

The gift is to understand. Stopping and sorting through all that we carry is for me one of the greatest and most important things we can do.

When we see that history is not the truth about us, we understand that this is the case with everyone. Even moms and dads.

Today, I feel a deep love for both my parents and my siblings.

Beyond our roles, we are all just vibrating love.

Make the most of your story. Dare to wake up and dare to see what is true.

There is a reconciliation exercise at the back of the book that you can easily use if you feel the need.

Client example

For many years I led ten-day primal courses, processes where you get to know your history and childhood. Those courses were incredible. For so many days, there is time to go deep and examine all that governs from the subconscious and be able to become aware of all the patterns that we have brought with us that we put on top of our own unique energy.

Watching people arrive on the first day and then seeing the happy free faces leaving the room. These were courses that transformed.

Today there are new simpler techniques that transform and make us aware in an incredibly powerful and simple way, for example Byron Katie's The Work or Family Constellations by Hellinger to untie old energy ties.

But also in my individual sessions, strong insights and transformations take place. With the help of the life wheel, many have dared to see their story for what it is.

I remember a woman who came to me.

The result of the story was that she was completely burned out by her family of origin.

Her marriage had collapsed because her mother needed her so much. She was very much 'married' to her mother.

Her mother's needs had come first in her whole life.

When we put pillows on the floor for everyone in the family and she had to stand in her place, in the middle of everything, to see what it looked like. She burst into tears, she could hardly breathe and everything became very clear to her.

She had taken on the role of mother's extended arm. She was there to be mom's emotional protection. She was there for her mother's needs. The mother wanted her life to come first.

It is so deeply rooted.

Laying out cushions to see the big picture more clearly helps people to understand and feel more easily. We worked on putting it right. A reconciliation work about letting go of the old thoughts to be able to grow up to be who she was now.

Become an adult. Let mom have her feelings and she herself have hers, no longer living in a symbiosis of dependency and confusion of energy.

When the woman saw and understood the whole picture and began to see who she was without this maternal bond, she felt so much love for her husband who had been pointing this out to her all these years. And she had denied it. The woman could see that it was her husband she was married to. Now she was an adult and it was not her mother with whom she would have that bond anymore.

Now she saw. She made contact with her ex-husband. Told him all the things she saw as the truth now. She thanked him and she could love him for who he was.

Their children, whom I have also met, have told me that their father broke up with his new wife and started courting their mother again.

They don't live together but have an incredibly friendly love for each other. She is just one of many who have been transformed over the years. Growing up more consciously, no longer having a bond like being 'married' to your mom or dad, is important for us to have good presence in our relationships.

Another example is women looking for a 'father'.

It becomes roles and can be difficult to feel the love that we are. If we had not had a father figure as a child. The security a father can be in a perfect world. This can be compensated for by seeking it in a relationship as adults. The man the woman meets becomes the father figure that never existed. But the man knows about it and he has his history. The relationship becomes messy and it becomes difficult to be who we are today.

Now we are adults, then, before we were a child. It is the child's needs and not the adult's that govern. If we become aware, we can behave in a completely different way.

Exercise

Write down your entire childhood history.
What was it like when you were born? What kind of scene were you born into and what role did you take or see yourself taking?

....

....

....

How has your history shaped you? See how it is reflected in your life today. What role did you play in your family?

....

....

....

Who would you be if history didn't control you anymore?
How would you live then?

....

....

....

Are you willing to start growing out of history and take care of and get to know the child you once were?

Are you willing to reconcile and start seeing your mom and dad for who they were? There is a little child inside them too but most likely they were not helped to see and understand.

....

....

....

What painful experiences have you been through in your life? Can you see how these turned off your life energy? How would you live if these events did not rule your life today?

....

....

....

What do you see that the gifts were in your childhood?

....

....

....

What do you need to do to grow up and reconcile with the different events of history?
If we don't, it's controlling us from the subconscious.

....

....

....

If you look at your whole family tree back in history. Where are the pains and emotions bound up?
Where has the energy stopped?

....

....

....

Where has love been in your life? Who have you felt seen by?

....

....

....

What did it look like when you were happy as a child? Describe as clearly as you can the qualities you see that you had as a child (which is still inside you).

....

....

....

What are your emotional memories from your childhood?

....

....

....

What have you learned from your story?

....

....

....

Who are you, free from your history and all the thoughts you carry from it?

....

....

Here in this now, who are you free from your history? What does your longing look like ?

Right now just rest in who you are....

Breathe in, breathe out, everything happens by itself and you can in this moment give yourself the freedom to just be...

Looking at history with some distance...

Executive summary

See history for what it is.

Here you were a child. Important to understand how you experienced it as a child.

Sort out and reconcile in the way that brings the energy back to the naturally true order. Allow acceptance and reconciliation with your parents to happen within you. Create peace within you.

You have a story, you are not your story.

It is for you to grow up and become an adult in, not to stay in.

The challenge

To reconcile and let go of history. Growing up and taking responsibility for your life.

Childhood is an important period in your life. Never have you been so vulnerable, open and dependent as then. Being able to see and bring this quality home to yourself is an important part of experiencing the wholeness within you.

The challenge is to be able to let go of the identification with what has happened and been there.

Allowing reconciliation to happen. Being able to embrace, feel the emotional memories that come up.

Understanding that the wounds activated often come from this period in our lives.

Hellinger's family constellations are extremely helpful to have as a tool here.

Primal therapy and breathing allow us to get below the surface and understand what lies in our subconscious.

The little child inside you and the story you carry needs to come home to yourself and your own heart. Otherwise, the story and unconsciousness will rule your life and all aspects of life. Awareness and love is what melts all misconceptions.

4. PROFESSIONAL ROLE

*T*o share and give of their unique quality and presence. We want to and we feel good about it.

Find the passion in what you do or find your passion and let it become your profession.

Respect for your own unique potential. Your inner life potential and creativity.

Finding a professional role in which we can grow and expand is important for most of us. When we live our professional role and give all our energy there, it is also important for us to be able to step out of the role, to be able to look at it from the outside. To see the part you have in the bigger picture. It's equally important to be able to step out of your professional role and just be with your friends. The balance between expanding and taking your potential seriously. Being able to just be and relax with your friends.

Learn to share your unique life energy and quality. The more love you can feel for yourself and the role you have, the truer and more harmonious you can live.

General

Finding meaning in life through work is something most of us need to do. For most of us, it's about making a living. But finding passion in what we do, living because we want to give of our unique energy, talents and gifts. Working just to make money makes for a very poor life. Your wealth is within you and when it comes to life, we feel rich.

To feel confident in who we are and what we have to contribute. As this is the only part we have been trained in, it can become the part we most identify with. Which can cause an imbalance. We can become workaholics, which in our world has unfortunately become increasingly common. Compulsively to reduce anxiety, emptiness, feelings of alienation, fear of not being good enough, seek confirmation and be able to feel power.

An area we can hide behind. Our ego takes over and we think that the professional role is who we are.

If we do not have confidence in ourselves, it is difficult to fully commit to our work.

Self-confidence or trust in what lives within us. Your unique qualities.

Many of us have studied and learned a lot of knowledge.

Or if you take energy from within and paint. Creating music. Dancing or writing, for example if you are an artistic soul. Even then we need to learn a certain knowledge. All inspiration comes from within. Musicians need to learn notes and an instrument. But then comes the personal feeling that is important through music.

There the feeling is allowed to participate and is an asset. It can do so in all other contexts too.

Unfortunately, many jobs do not have a high status. But they need to exist and then you can see that what you contribute is an important part of the whole society.

We believe that we are this role that we have. We believe that some professional roles are more important than others.

Everything is connected. We are a web of different important tasks to be performed.

Our profession and our role are part of a wider context. Our society.

And our world.

When we think we are our role, and think it is more important than everyone else's. This creates an imbalance.

We are all equally important. We all have different roles and it's good to step out of role to just hang out with friends or just be.

You are important, your role is important and the deeper contact you have with yourself, the more in tune you can be.

About me

In my life, there has never been a clear idea of what I should do for a living. I know that there are many hidden creative talents within me. Among other things, there is an unfulfilled architect. As a child, I would lie in bed before going to sleep and invent different types of houses that I built in nature. Decorated in the most amazing ways. Houses with their interiors blended in with the nature they were in. When I look at those ideas today, I can only feel great wonder. I played the piano as a child at the age of seven and as it seemed, I was quite good. But it all ended on the day of a concert in a large auditorium. I was playing four hands with a boy. The hall was full of parents and friends. However, none of my family came. I remember how the steps down from the stage felt. After that day I never played again. Creativity and joy were replaced by sadness. I didn't understand then what was happening. Pretended that I would rather ride. Horses came in for a while but they too disappeared. Creativity is something that came naturally to me. But emotions of various kinds meant that it did not come out or was turned off more and more. I am not unique in this.

Early on I wanted to work in my life. Got a job in the summer kiosk. Advanced the following summer to work in the bakery. An incredibly fun summer month. It smelled good and everyone who shopped was on vacation and happy. Those who came loved the bread and all the buns. It was a taste of working with something where people were happy that we existed. That my job contributed to happy people. I loved that feeling when I got on my bike early every summer morning to ride to work.

My mother, who was a trained dental nurse, was proud of her education and had told me early on that I should work and feel that I could manage on my own and stand on my own two feet. But she wasn't there, which created confusion in me.

So I turned to my dad.

My first career choice when I was about fifteen was to become a lawyer.

"No, you'll never make it. Have you seen how thick the law book is? You'll never make it."

Doctors were my next. "No, you won't be able to handle all the blood."

I was good at math and a bit of a pedant. Architect, I think would have suited me perfectly. A sense of beauty has also always been there.

"No, you need sharp elbows for that. You're far too sensitive."

Well, there wasn't much hope left of that.

I realized that, in my father's eyes, my talents were zero. That was how he related to himself and his inner creativity and wealth. I didn't realize at the time how easy I had it with certain things; among other things, I could also sew my own clothes early on.

My inner life was rich. And it feels like I had confidence in it early in life. But when I didn't get the support that it's possible to realize inner talents, the potential stayed inside. This meant that my dreams disappeared faster than they came. I also lost my faith in the future when my mother left the family. And then when she died, all my longing was locked deep down inside me.

When others went to career counseling, I went home.

I had given up. My feeling was that there was no point anyway.

I don't think my father understood what he was saying to me. He was born in 1908 and was forty-seven years old when I was born and had a completely different idea of what women's role in life should be. Something I saw and understood much later in life.

He was fully aware of the power of what he was saying.

Fortunately, it opened the door to my intuition. It has helped me find my way.

And it took me on a completely different journey.

Before I found myself and my inner world, I worked as a clothing buyer. I was the responsible buyer at a big department store for seven years. A career without goals or vision. After my awakening and after clearing out my entire life wheel, then life took another turn.

At first, I took jobs just to make a living. I wanted to travel to India and spend as much time there as possible to meditate and learn the wisdom of mindful presence. My energy and focus was to get rooted within myself and in the present moment beyond my own thinking about how life should be. To meet people in a presence. To look openly and lovingly at another individual. To be able to affirm and trust what is. To be able to sort out what has been in order to live a life in more presence, love and openness. After the seven years, life took me into the next role. Leading courses and helping people sort out their inner life. I am still on that journey. It is intuition and life that guides and guides. Life shows the way. I float along.

Mullingstorp kursgård, at that time one of Sweden's largest course farms in personal development, came as the first step in starting to lead courses. Which I did for six years. That gift came to me.

Then Lars Vedam Knutsson came and asked if I wanted and could help them start a new course farm that he and his wife had just bought. That gift also came without any action on my part.

I helped with BaraVara's vision. That people could have more love in their lives. There I created many different courses in individual development. The most successful and their base is the Door Opening processes that I both created and led during the almost seven years I was there. The Door Opening courses became and still are a highly appreciated course process.

Both at Mullingstorp's course center and in all the creation of building BaraVara and the courses there, there has been an unconscious energy from my history in me, of being guided by 'being there to help my dad'. I am and have been focused on my dad's needs. Dad needing me and me giving all that I have but nothing coming back. My patterns of growing up with only my father and focusing on his well-being, I have unconsciously dragged with me in the work context. Both Bengt Stern and Vedam Lars Knutsson have been such 'father figures' in my life. There's nothing wrong with that, it's just that we reflect our history in different ways throughout our lives. He was there for me. My emotional wounds were difficult for me to express. Which was not his job to understand. That was and is my responsibility. That said, our collaboration was one of great love and respect.

Being true to my inner self, it has guided me. To live in the moment. Giving everything and trusting that life is there to support us. Expansion happens naturally. The next step happens when it should. It just is.

Remember that once a long time ago, when I was just starting my "new" life, that an astrologer said to me " You Lena can't live to just create money. It will not work. You can only live and dare to follow your heart. That is your only chance".

He has been right.

Whatever the case, it is my inner self that has guided me, not the other way around.

What I have worked with is to guide and help people to find home and understand themselves. To be able to sort out and find love for themselves and their lives. To be able to transform the inner world we have so that our outer life can be lived in more love and awareness. I believe that also to begin to allow the inner creative energies in the form of creation in different ways also want to get more space. This book is an example. It feels to me like there is more that is waiting in there. To allow the natural expansion that lives in there. We all have it in different ways.

Client example.

One of my clients, Anette, came to me because she never managed to keep her jobs.

She had worked as an administrator and project manager.

Again and again, she had the same experience.

She had a falling out with her boss, especially if it was a woman.

Her self-confidence was at rock bottom.

When she came to me, she was on sick leave for burnout and depression.

We started to look at her whole situation, all the parts of the wheel of life. How it had been, that made her find herself where she was right now. She cried a lot and felt useless. Then we looked at what she was wearing.

Her mother had been in hospital a lot during her childhood.

Anette, who was an only child, had supported and been there for her. She had taken a lot of the responsibility. Her father had worked and also been there for her mother. But his energy at home and towards her mother, as Anette saw it as a child, was that he pushed her down and did not understand how fragile his wife was.

Anette was both proud that she had found a job that supported her, but also troubled by anger towards her boss. Which in this case was a mixture of the image of her mother and father. She wanted to be accommodating but at the same time there was an energy that wanted to say no, enough is enough, other people will have their way with me.

The more we saw how her childhood and the role she had taken on then, had been the guiding energy she had brought to work, the easier it was. When she saw, she could understand.

Her reconciliation with herself and the history she carried could begin.

And she could see her job role for what it was. What challenges and expansion opportunities were there.

Her boss had to become a boss with the role that it implied, she could respect that. She could behave like an adult. Not be like the disappointed child she had previously identified with.

She had clear responsibilities in her professional role. She became an adult.

She was looking forward to meeting and being able to see her boss and her professional role in an adult way. It was there that she could see herself growing beyond the anger and ambiguity.

Another client, a man named Gustav, came to me because he could never feel satisfied with himself in what he did and achieved.

His boss had asked him to come to me for support in understanding himself better.

In his case, there was an incredibly demanding father in the family of origin. It was always the father's achievements that counted, not what the boy had done.

He remembered how they had played football when he was little. His father and him. The neighbors had always said "What a nice dad who goes out and plays with his son so much".

In the boy's world it was different. He had been extremely happy when his father took his hand and said "Let's go out, just you and me, and play some football".

Happy and cheerful, the game began.

But as soon as the little boy got to the ball, the father came and kicked it. Then he ran again towards the ball. And when the boy was almost there, the father came and kicked it again. No matter how hard he tried, he never made it all the way to the ball before his dad stylishly kicked it away. His "good" dad had kicked the ball just before he got there each time.

He never touched the ball. These football incidents often happened during a period when the boy was between three and four years old. In the end, the boy no longer wanted to play and chose another sport where his father had no chance.

The father's need to constantly assert himself and the boy's desire to be seen were reflected in his work today. It was as if he was walking with a big sign in front of him "See me, see me! I am good. I can do it".

The focus was on being seen and being acknowledged, instead of getting to know his own capacity and being happy with it. He was incredibly capable. But he couldn't see it himself.

After some time with me, he was offered a management job. He accepted the challenge.

I think his role as a manager is extremely stimulating for him and I think that as a manager he is responsive to his staff.

He knows how it feels.

Exercise

What is your current work situation?
What thoughts and feelings do you see that guide you?

....

....

....

What role have you taken in your professional life?

....

....

....

How would you like it to be? Dare to be true, it's your life.

....

....

....

Trust in your talents... Which ones do you see that you have? What is it like for you to be true?

....

....

....

What can you do to get out of your own way so that your talents can have space and expand?

....

....

....

Executive summary

Seeing the difference between your role and who you are.

Becoming aware of how history haunts the present. It's not the creativity that's the problem. It's the feelings of non-value you put on top of it that are.

What you have not sorted out within yourself is reflected in your work situation.

Becoming aware of how history is reflected in your current situation. The only thing is to see. Nothing more. When you see, change happens by itself as it should. What a wonderful school to grow in. You work, get paid and increase your awareness. Change happens when it should, if it should.

Increase your presence and awareness.

Take your life in your hands. Working together means that two people meet in acceptance and share their creativity. Where both or all qualities are equally important. As an organism where everything works together. Become aware of what you contribute.

Create a conscious atmosphere together with your colleagues.

Conscious leadership groups no matter what we do.

If each person is given access to their capacity and unique qualities, we create a functioning organism. From organization to healthy functioning organism where every part and individual is important with its wisdom and energy.

In all the organizations I have worked in, it has been my job to give the individual awareness of their own characteristics to be able to see the common power. To be able to appreciate it and see that it can be bigger than all the separate parts of life. Everyone is important.

In leadership development, know in depth who you are as a leader. If you can lead yourself, you can lead others.

The challenge

To grow, to allow your qualities and talents to flourish, without letting your ego take the credit.

The ego is your false self. The part that often rules our lives before we have truly examined who we are.

The ego is based on the story of us. The ego wants something from the outside, while our inner nature wants to give of itself.

The ego is the learned while our inner self is living life potential. Love your unique inner qualities, let them give their unique quality. Open your inner doors. Like a seed that longs to burst open and start growing.

The ego is like writing on the seed that it is a rose. But when the shell cracks open, the real rose can bloom. It is in harmony with all divinity.

One challenge is to truly reconcile what stands in the way of your unique expression coming to life. There is only one of you and that is you. Live her or him as truly and lovingly as you ever can. Find confidence in yourself. Listen and dare to act one step at a time. Get help and support.

Let your life potential and inner creativity come to the surface and to life. The next aspect of the Wheel of Life helps you to trust more.

5. LIFE VISION, DIRECTION IN LIFE AND LONGING

*D*are to say yes to living and to realizing your longing. Desire lives in your heart and one step at a time, without losing the present, it shows you the way. Say yes!

The bigger the picture, the easier it is to understand and live.

The power that lives in the present takes *us* where we are going!

To have an intention with your life. To dare to see your own direction. To dare to dream big and have confidence that it is possible.

The power of the present is the same as your longing. We must stay in the present and have roots there. But to dare to look up and see "what do I want with my life?".

Experiencing and living happiness is one of the visions we all have.

Life vision is finding your focus. To trust the feeling you have.

Knowing here and now what to do to go in my and life's direction.

Find and listen to your longing. It is the direction of your life. Your longing lives in your heart. Listen there.

General

Rarely, if ever, do we ask ourselves "What do I want with my life?"

It's not so much about where I want to go or where I'm going. More about finding confidence in life.

One day this form of life will end.

It is more about how do I want to live. What is my longing. What does it look like.

Healing happens when we take our lives into our own hands.

By life vision I mean the focus we have right now.

It is difficult to rest in the present if I do not have confidence that what is to happen will come to me. When I do not dare to believe that it is possible.

To rest in the present is to trust that the next now will be loving. How can my life be better?

What can I do to flourish in my life. What am I longing for?

How do I want to feel on the day when life's journey is coming to an end?

About me

In my case, before I started to know myself, there was no faith in the future. Nor was there any contact with that which knows and guides me from within. There was only an inner turmoil, something that chafed. A spiritual longing, something diffuse that I could not figure out. It was nothing in the outer world that I longed for. It was in the inner world. It was the inner longing that then woke up more and more and eventually took me on a completely different journey. I asked the people I had around me at the time if they had the same inner wounds. If they were happy with what was. If they felt an inherent power that wanted to come out.

"No, I don't feel that", I was told.

I was going crazy myself.

I did everything to make this force subside. I wanted to be like everyone else. I wanted to be normal. Like a normal human being who didn't have weird internal abrasions. What I didn't know then was that this force was my inner life potential. That it was me, my history and unconsciousness that stood in the way.

Desire was my unique inner quality. It was this energy that had its own wisdom and knew where it was going. To say yes and affirm that power is to live with life. To say no and shut that power away is to live in pain.

In my life, power has guided me. I have followed it on this exciting journey.

In the present is the intuitive force that takes us in the right direction and to the next now.

My life vision is and was to live in trust.

Embracing all the challenges and gifts that life brings.

Living in the present.

To live in a yes. To dare to expand.

Living in harmony with life.

To just listen to my inner self.

To dare to love when it comes my way. To live and have a loving true relationship with myself and life.

To listen and say yes. To follow and trust in life itself.

To dare to say yes when I mean yes, and no when I mean no.

On the day this life ends, I want to feel that I am letting go and allowing the next step to happen in love and trust. I want to feel that I have done what I should and lived openly. That I dared to accept all challenges. Dared to love. Dared to live. Dared to be me. Dared to just be.

My dreams start now. And now and now. I love having visions and dreams. They don't take me away, they take me here. For example, if I have an inner feeling that I should go out into the world and do a course, or meditate or meet people I haven't seen for a long time. Then I trust that feeling. I often meditate first and let my inner self guide me. I know that my inner longing and life itself have the same longing, which gives me confidence. I then take one step at a time and let life guide me. All the time I am in the present. I am anchored in the present, I let myself take each step as it should. Trusting and in the present. The vision that I feel comes from within. It is the inner life potential that lives there.

It wants to expand in its own way. I embrace it. When a dream or vision is fulfilled, I continue to live in the present. I do not linger. The experience and what I experienced is in my experience bank. Living in the moment and letting go of your dreams gives you a sense of ownership of your life. To be your own best friend who wants the best for you. Life becomes a wonderful journey with yourself. To live free from baggage. To be able to live present and open in trust in what happens and what life wants.

Under this heading also comes the vision of life we all know but almost never talk about. The fact that we know we will leave this earthly life one day. We all share it. We are going back to the place we once came from. Like a leaf falling to the ground when the time comes. I have asked myself many times what I would like it to look like. What is clear to me is that I want to feel that I have lived and said yes to what life has given me, not held back but dared to take the steps to be taken. In love.

I want to surround myself with friends who support this next step in leaving and saying goodbye. To hold the hand of a dear friend. Allowing my curiosity and alertness to accompany me in this process if possible.

I don't know how it will work out, but I'm getting used to the idea of it. That life can be in the sign of meditation, presence here and now makes me train for the final challenge when that day comes.

Client example

Pain that we carry can have its different causes.

Pain of a painful childhood.

Pain over the roles in life not working.

But there will also be those who have a clear spiritual pain.

A pain where the unique inner longing and potential for life has not been expressed.

To say yes to your life.

That the roles and social patterns keep the energy locked in a compartment.

What do you want from your life?

Often this question comes to the surface when we have reached a certain stage in life.

One of my clients, a woman who worked. Had three children. A relatively good marriage.

"Why am I not feeling well?"

"I feel like I'm not living the life I should".

"My children, my husband, my friends think I should just relax but I can't."

She had an incredible quality and power that she locked away.

A force that was loving. A force that wanted something with her.

She said yes! The journey that began for her was a bit shaky at first. She did not know where it would lead.

Her husband was worried. Her children were worried. But she had no other choice.

One step at a time, she acknowledged her longing.

The work we did together was to highlight how she wanted to live her life.

What qualities. How she wanted to feel, how she wanted to be with her family, but mostly how she wanted to start listening to herself and her inner silent voice. To dare to follow and trust her awareness.

It was clear to her that she wanted to live with an open heart.

That she wanted to live in a yes to expand.

That she was now done with this old way of life, that she had done and accepted the challenges that had come to her.

It was her life vision.

She lives with her longing. She trusts her longing. One step at a time.

Today, both her husband and children are lovingly included in her various projects.

Of course, this is not always the case. But for her, family cohesion became stronger. It had to do with the fact that we worked on putting into words and being clear about what her longing was about. That she could put into words and explain to her dear family what she was going through. She loved her family, her family with husband and children loved her.

She needed to learn to listen to her inner strong longing so that it would be given space in her life. She was grateful for it. So, if you have an inner longing that's nagging you, start listening to it.

Dare to listen to the inner silent voice that lives within us. In my case, this power was so clear, but I had no understanding of what it was. Just like a seed that has its inner potential and just longs to burst open and start sprouting to be able to realize itself. So it is with us, I also think my mother had a strong longing for life. Whatever her childhood years, there was a yearning for 'something more'. Which led her to leave our father and start a whole new life when she was forty-nine. She moved out into the world, Africa and Asia. Learning English, having a staff of servants, something she had not planned but it was all part of the new life for her.

It just happened to be the way it was. But I think it was the inner longing she had that made her dare or feel compelled to go regardless of the circumstances.

Exercise

What are you longing for in your life? The voice of longing is silent, so give yourself time to just rest in that stillness.

....

....

....

How do you want to live your life?

....

....

....

When your life is coming to an end and you can look back on your life. How do you want to feel that you have lived your life?

With what quality do you want to leave this life? Can you start living it today?

....

....

....

What do you feel you can do to achieve your aspirations, dreams and life vision?

....

....

....

Executive summary

In the present is the power that leads you to the next now.

Dare to live with it.

Dare to say yes beyond your own limitations.

The desire and the life force are already there.

Dare to listen to your own dreams. Again and again. Don't let yourself stop. Let yourself live all that you feel is true, right and proper for you.

The challenge

To be able to say yes to the natural expansion that wants to happen, anchored in the present.

The inner longing is the same as life's, there is no separation between life and you. When you start to say yes, you will see that life is there and supports every step you take.

Dare to dream big but realize that it is in the present that the dream can begin.

You are the one who can make the dream come true. That journey starts here and now!

Dream big. Let all your limitations step aside. Say yes! And let life guide you.

We are here to find home in love and in our true nature. Dare to give yourself a life in harmony with happiness, truth and wholeness. See the present and trust your inner creative life potential.

6. LOVE RELATIONSHIP

*T*o dare to live with an open heart. To receive the true reflections that we get in a love relationship. Two people who are open and filled with love energy who want to share and be true, or two people filled with old programs who want to rule and be right?

When we fall in love at the beginning of a relationship, we are completely pure and open to the other person. We often have no programs that get in the way. Our heart is just a big open yes. Attraction has arisen between two energies. No one but the two people in the relationship know the mystery between them. But as wonderful as it can be, it is also a challenge. Often after it's been a while, our subconscious comes in and all the ideas thoughts, the chaos that we carry come in and start to rule and speak about how the partner "should" be. Our hearts are then no longer in a yes but start to close up in a feeling that we would rather be right than be loving. Our old story comes in and gets in the way. Then comes the challenge to start seeing that aspect of ourselves. It's not you relating to your partner anymore. The partner has changed and we start projecting someone else onto our partner. It is often our primal story that is mirrored up, like mom, dad who thus stands between you and the partner, you and the love here and now, you and your open heart.We all long for love, to expand and to give. To live and melt together. To blur our boundaries. To be one with something bigger than ourselves. It can happen on many different levels. But if I can't love myself, it's hard to let someone else love me and it's hard to love someone. Allowing ourselves to live lovingly in a relationship requires us to work on increasing our awareness. Out of that always comes love. It is our nature. But if we stay unconscious, it is difficult. Then love becomes like playing the lottery. Maybe it will come. The love, the energy I'm talking about is the true, natural energy we are all made of. And the only thing that can stop it is unconsciousness. To be able to step out of the way, to begin to understand what it is that prevents it from flowing is the only job we need to do. That possibility lives in you and within you. We are all love.

Either you feel in your heart that you want to be with your partner or you don't. Only you know that. But either way, it's never your partner who is the problem, it's in you.

If you want to live with your partner, learn to live lovingly and truly together. Most of us need help in our relationships. Partly to see what is old that haunts us, and learn how to live lovingly. Create a platform of trust and growth. We have not learned to live in love. To understand who we are as a man or woman. To understand the opposite sex.

If you don't want to be with your partner, take responsibility for it. Being in a relationship and feeling like you don't really want to be there only creates pain for both of you.

The mystery of love between two people is of the greatest value. A human being comes into your life and a new universe is born. We had no idea that this person existed, nor do we know what this meeting will give and teach us.

Keeping our hearts open so they don't dam up again is the job of any relationship.

Do we want encounters in the present or do we want our stories to fit together? When our stories meet, no true encounter can happen. Only our stories collide or interact.

A true meeting between individuals is a meeting when we are empty and can be present with each other in the moment. Love is not "I love you if you just change yourself to be better based on my ideas". Love is when we can be present without the expectation of wanting to change the other. Love is the energy that already exists and brought you together to this meeting.

Your relationship is your perfect mirror. Being able to give and receive love.

No relationship is better than the relationship you have with yourself. Most of us enter relationships because we want something. We want our partner to see and give us what we feel we need. It can be a codependency. But the truth is that the only way to be able to keep a relationship alive and healthy is for you to be in a relationship to be able to give. To give love instead of getting. Give the love you have. Then the relationship becomes a living relationship where love makes you rich. Then the relationship becomes a meeting between two givers who help each other grow, come home and become more of themselves.

The inner communication reflected in the outer.

In every man there is an inner woman and in every woman there is an inner man.

We come from a man and a woman. Both of those qualities are in us. We are the whole. The mirroring with the opposite partner allows us to start seeing and understanding our counterpart.

If we feel for a moment that the external relationship mirrors the encounter that is within you.

What does the inner meeting look like. Are both your inner male and inner female energies given space? Is there respect between them?

Projections can help us become whole or they can separate us.

We are whole people, we have everything inside us. We have different roles. Love relationships are one of the most important ones that many of us have. And we have almost never been taught about that area of our lives. Boys have never been taught the difference between them and girls. And girls have never been taught about boys. And we have never been taught that we are the whole. Being able to understand and get to know oneself is an important challenge in life. To begin to melt and be able to reflect oneself in an external relationship. It is a wonderful gift but also a journey to learn about yourself. Your relationship reflects how you relate to yourself on the inside.

The foundation is a good relationship with yourself and life.

Learn to live and share love. It is the greatest of gifts to yourself and your partner.

In love there is no right or wrong. Only what is true.

When we're teenagers, our hormones start to mess around in our bodies. Sexuality starts to come alive inside us. It starts to take a direction towards another person. If as children we lived and were whole and innocent and lived our inner quality, here at about 14 perhaps for the first time the energy begins to be directed towards another person. Since we usually have not received any training in our energy system, we begin to mix up love and sexuality.

I see it as the love between two people is like a garden. A garden that needs to be cared for and nurtured. What we grow grows. Weeds come and we can see together what needs to be done to remove the weeds. We can create this garden together. It is a joint effort what kind of garden we want. We are often so controlled by our history that we don't have the energy or understanding of what we want to create. We hope that the energy and attraction we feel when we meet will carry us forward forever. As if we had nothing to do with it. Having a vibrant love relationship, with all that it entails, is work. A work to keep it clean, to keep it alive so that "weeds" don't take over.

The energy meeting of our bodies

- In understanding that we are divine energy.
- Listening and trusting your intuition and yours.
- The art of communication and spontaneity in relationships.
- Unconditional love.
- Everyone owns their power in balance.
- In touch with their feelings and opening the door of the senses.
- The fire of sexuality. A yes to meeting your partner here.

We are mirrored in each other.

What does it look like when the energy flows between us as a couple, when we are open to each other?

When we understand our layers of energy that we carry within us, our relationships can expand and grow incredibly beautifully. A love relationship is so much more than just sexual attraction. As all energy does, we attract the partner that mirrors ourselves in different ways.

One quality can be trust. Are we nurturing that quality?
One quality can be to listen
Emotional closeness
Common time
Communication

Sex and attraction are often the start of a relationship. But the needs of sexuality change over the years. It often looks different for women and men.

The woman often needs emotional closeness and then comes her sexual desire. The man may need a sexual encounter in order to feel emotional closeness.

For our energy to flow, we need to keep our hearts open.

In order to keep your heart open, you need to constantly land at home in yourself. Allowing air to be between you as a couple. To communicate about what is happening between you. Not letting too much time pass with unspoken truths. The energy needs to be alive and flowing between you. When we understand that what the partner awakens in us has nothing to do with him or her. It is part of your story. The history you have with your emotional memories is something you need to take responsibility for. In most cases, relationships start out as lovely, open and loving.

Then the wounds and our history start to activate. "You're just like my mom" or "You look like my dad. He also locked his feelings inside". Becoming aware that you are the one projecting your story onto your partner. Sort it out so that your role with your partner can be as pure true and loving as possible. Otherwise, we slowly turn off our energy and the love that lives there between us.

Keeping the heart alive is the gift to yourself and your partner.

If we have an account for money at work, we can also create "accounts" in our relationships. An account of invested energy that creates trust. An account that creates emotional closeness. An account where we give energy and love to each other. When we only want to have, when we only want the partner to understand and give, then the energy account is emptied quite quickly and the relationship becomes negative.

When I've worked with couples, it's so clear that we take for granted that we can use our partner to "dump" our emotions and anger on. Where does that stand? Where did we learn that?

We work on setting up accounts for the qualities we want our relationship to have. Once we have deposited into the different accounts, then we can withdraw. Argue. Speak truths. Otherwise, the energy in your relationship will be misused, you will take out more than you put in.

Get a love account with your partner.

A trust account. What does it look like? What can give you more trust

A trust account with yourself and your surroundings. It is difficult to have a loving relationship if we do not trust each other and ourselves.

Helping each other to grow. Become more of yourselves. Not less. Start making time to have love meetings where you get to know each other.

About me

My relationships have really reflected where I have been with myself. I've been able to clearly see how my history has been reflected here. The patterns of mom not being there for me. When she was there it was amazing but the next moment she was completely gone. My patterns with my dad. That my needs are not important, but his needs are most important so that his pain does not surface. I feel blessed that I have seen and become aware of this. At the core of me there is a trust and a yes to what comes to me. So when love has come my way, I have said yes from day one! I have thrown myself into the unknown again and again. I have learned the hard way. But for me it has been the school of life that I grow with. The pain that has been the price has been a healing and a gift to myself and my own growth. Love itself heals and challenges us. Maybe not in the way we thought, but where love is, there is also our growth potential. It embraces us and it makes us just have to expand, include and forgive and reconcile.

In the beginning it was just hormones. I didn't have a healthy female role model when I entered my teens.

As I have written before, my mother did not like her body, so neither did I. I just had a body that was filled with sadness, loss and insecurity. However, this was not entirely true as I can remember that in moments I could experience that I liked myself from the inside.

I was lucky enough to have a boyfriend who was extremely loving and sensitive. We were both wounded in different ways. His father had died a few years earlier. And my mother had disappeared further and further away. We didn't talk about it, but that energy was there between us.

We were together for a few years when I was sixteen to nineteen.

He was an extremely good support to me during that time.

Things were a bit messy with relationships for some time after that. When I was with my mother in Jakarta and Indonesia, I was with a young ship owner, a Norwegian who had his life in the family shipping business. I liked him because he knew my mother and that it was luxury and abundance. But when things started to get serious, I saw that this was not for me. I longed to feel love on a deeper level. Even though both my mom and dad tried to make me understand that I didn't know or understand what love was. I trusted myself there and broke up with them. I was young and had my life ahead of me.

But when my mother died, I was more or less shut down inside, which was reflected in my relationships. Today I cannot understand how I and the man I married related.

I was completely numb, sad, scared and angry.

He hadn't cut the umbilical cord with his mother, but was more "married" to her than to me.

We were only married for three years. When he started talking about having children, I panicked.

I was unfaithful. I was getting attention from another man.

I couldn't stop it. And I couldn't tell you.

Tried on a few occasions but it didn't work. Everything ended with a bang. I left with more debt than I brought in.

It was all my fault, I thought.

Then it became a bit tentative.

History repeated itself but instead of finding another man to relate to, the turning point in my life came. I looked inside myself and the relationship with myself changed. I began to understand what patterns I had with myself. That I had not liked myself. How could anyone else? The patterns from my childhood and what had happened had ruled my whole life. The man I had moved in with met me when I was married. I had been unfaithful in all my seclusion. Now that I started to open up and fell "in love" with myself. When my inner journey had freed me, he got scared. His control mechanisms no longer worked. I also had no words for what had happened to me. I did not understand the dimensions. He was used to being able to control me, now that it was no longer possible, he became completely insane. His anger took over completely and we had horror scenarios and dramas. He tried to strangle me, he locked me up. He threw whiskey glasses at me at parties when no one was looking. His locked-up anger took its toll on me. He was no longer able to control himself.

I realized that we had not had a love affair but a control affair. He had controlled me. Now it was no longer possible. I was no longer there as I had been before. In his world, he thought I had found someone else. It was true, I had found myself and the whole with it. His anger knew no bounds. At one point he called Bengt Stern, the doctor who had recommended that I start working on myself.

He called me and said "I'm going to kill myself, it's your fault. Just so you know". Bengt's response was, "If you can wait until Wednesday, I have another option. I will have my first course in a hotel in Stockholm, come there and look into yourself instead". So he did. He went for Bengt on his first course. I was not aware of this at the time. I had already moved and relocated.

There was no turning back for me. There were too many patterns of unconsciousness between us and I didn't want to go any further. It was over.

After that, my love journey with myself began to deepen. Relating with men became secondary. I love freedom. And I have chosen not to have children because I never wanted anyone to feel the way I did. For long periods of my life, I just needed to be with myself.

It has allowed me on my journey to follow love as it happened and I have been able to follow what has been true. I have learned so much through all my relationships. Been able to see patterns from my history.

Today, I have the best of friendships with several of my men. But the most important one is with myself. Being able to just be with myself. Learning to spend time with myself. That that relationship can be the main relationship. In that relationship there may or may not be a partner. I have learned so much about myself through each relationship. It's really clear how life gives us exactly what we need to grow.

Before I met the man I had lived with the longest, I made an inner journey with a process that OSHO created for us women, but also for men.

Women's liberation or Man's liberation.

It is about first meeting the collective energy that we carry as women/ men. To deeply see and understand. A permissive process of going into all the old imprints that we carry. Then allowing to start feeling and experimenting with our opposite sex, or the energy we otherwise do not live. I myself was many different male characters. This journey was so incredibly valuable and gave me a deep sense of what it is like to be a man. It was like I stepped into different eras and a lot of wisdom came out. One woman told me after the course that what I had talked about as a male doctor was of utmost value. She worked as a doctor and recognized my language. Very interesting to see how we can step into different types of energy and find so much wisdom.

After these two steps, one by one we were transformed into goddesses. Then it was a true liberation.

To see and understand that everything is there within us.

For me, after this process, meeting a man became something completely new, all contempt disappeared and the belief that the male energy was only on the outside of me no longer existed. All women carry an inner man, all men carry an inner woman. When these two energies meet within us, a union takes place. It makes us whole and enlightened. This in turn produces relationships where both can be as they are and rest in the divine wholeness.

A partner comes into life, love makes us grow and learn. Then when that's done, it's time to stop with oneself. Then comes the next one. I certainly haven't sought love in a man but life has wanted me to grow and I accept those gifts. All my relationships I am extremely grateful for. My life vision is to live true and be able to follow my heart. I have no children as my inner child needed all my attention to heal. For you it might be different. You always need to have your own overall picture to start from.

That we as individuals agree to give love to each other. Two friends who wish each other well. Two individuals helping each other to live lovingly.

All my relationships have been perfect. It was not their job to love me. It was mine. And each relationship has reflected perfect parts of myself that I could never have seen otherwise.

The illusion every time I fell in love was something completely different from what I was taught. My heart and love have expanded beyond anything I thought.

All infatuations are a gift to expand in and to grow in love.

Falling in love, feeling attraction, is a divine trick so that we can learn to grow beyond what we already know. In early years, perhaps, for us to procreate. But more is needed if our hearts are to expand.

Own and take responsibility for your own story

Thinking about yourself

Seeing the partner for who he or she is.

A willingness to grow together.

Male energy. A more active energy.

Female energy. More receptive energy.

All men have a receptive and feminine side.

All women have an inner male part.

This internal balance is often reflected in the external relationship.

Client example.

I have met many couples over the years. But one couple in particular stands out in my mind for their courage to stay put even when it was hard and not entirely obvious to them.

Anita and Lennart were both just over forty years old. Lennart had contacted me because he wanted a divorce. But he was too insecure and afraid to bring up and even talk about the situation. As always when I work with a couple, I want to meet the individuals one by one first.

Lennart immediately booked an appointment for himself. When he arrived, we looked at his current situation, what his childhood had been like and what he longed for, and how he would like it to be if it was optimal in his life.

Lennart talked about growing up as a child of divorce. He told how he saw his mother and father relate to each other. He could see that he had taken the same role as his mother. The mother had allowed herself to be pushed down by Lennart's father, her husband. My client had done the same in his relationship with his wife. He had felt that she had had the upper hand from the very beginning of their relationship. Another reflection that became clear was that Lennart was eleven years old when his parents separated. Lennart and his wife had two children, a boy and a girl. Their girl was the oldest and had just turned thirteen and their son would soon be eleven. He would be the same age as Lennart had been when his parents separated. He was amazed at the reflections that emerged so early. It was he who wanted a divorce, not his wife.

Anita also came to an individual session. In her case it was different. Her parents were still married. They had had their ups and downs but had never left each other. Anita was a driven, strong woman who loved her husband and appreciated his softer side. What she saw she had not managed to bring out in herself.

When they both arrived and we sat together, they had to tell us what reflections they saw from their own childhood. They had to start communicating with each other based on what they felt and could see. Lennart saw that he did not want to follow his mother and father's pattern, partly because he wanted to find his true path, partly because his mother had become a bitter old lady. He didn't want to be like that. Now that he and Anita were sharing themselves with each other in a whole new way, they decided to get to know each other on a deeper level. To become friends and want to understand each other.

Lennart's challenge was to start expressing his feelings and not suppress them. To become more clear and firm with his truths. Anita's challenges were to stop and be more present. To take in and dare to receive more of what Lennart wanted to give in the form of softness, presence and conversation. Both agreed to give the relationship a year. If it didn't work out, they would separate and work on being good parents. To be able to separate in a loving way.

Anita had been unfaithful once at the beginning of their relationship, which left a deep mark on Lennart. So building trust became important and each became more clear about who they were. The relationship started to have many peaks and troughs. They could both see how their stories and their egos would steer them in a destructive direction. While the love that was and had been there wanted something completely different. They wanted to be true and they wanted to grow. They wanted to be a family. And they wanted to find the passion again.

Lennart, who was more of a seeker, wanted to find new ways. That was not really Anita's energy.

They traveled to tantra courses, they started meditating together.

It is now five years since they came to me. They lived together for another four or five years after that. Then they separated. That separation was loving and filled with respect. The children, who have grown up, were involved in a completely different way with what happened to Lennart. They now live quite close together. There is still a lot of respect and love

During my years at Mullingstorp kursgård, I led a course, a three-step process in facing oneself. Step one was to meet oneself, step two was to come to terms with one's history. I was a co-creator of steps two and three. The third step I led and created myself in the last years. That step focused on self-love, loving oneself beyond the story and practicing meeting others in a loving presence. I had then added a meditation every evening that I called "Evening date meditation".

The idea was that you had to draw cards to decide who you would have a meeting with for one hour.

At the beginning of the week, most people were a little unsure and scared. Who would it be for the evening? What would happen? But with each day, more and more trust happened. Confidence in oneself. Trust in the person you had the date with. There was more and more love in the air. Everyone started to make themselves more and more beautiful. To practice being present. To be true to oneself. To feel what this particular meeting wanted. It was all very innocent and beautiful. They took walks, drank tea and talked or sat and meditated, gave each other healing. After this hour we met and shared the experiences. Everyone grew. One may add here that all had attended courses to sort out their old baggage of feelings and thoughts that had been in the way of a more loving and conscious life.

To start having open, present meetings with your partner. Having your own time together is extremely valuable, without demands. Only with a loving presence, trust and in truth. Getting to know yourself and your partner with the needs that exist.

The presence we give to our meetings, the love we give to our meetings is the quality that can never disappear or die. Only the story and my thoughts about how it should be, can die away.

Exercise

What have your relationships looked like for you over the years? What have you learned through them?
Have they reflected your history? Your mom or dad?

....

....

....

Do you trust your own gender? Do you trust the opposite sex?

....

....

....

What does it mean to you to be there for your partner? Can you be open, supportive and present for your partner?

....

....

....

How does it look today? What are your thoughts and feelings?

....

....

....

What would you like it to look like?

....

....

....

How is your history reflected in your relationship or non-relationship?

....

....

....

What do you need to do to create what you long for?
With or without a partner. You can be the one you have been longing for.
What do you need to give to yourself today to show that you respect and
love yourself and can accept your partner.

....

....

....

What are your romantic ideas? What turns you on and increases your
attraction to a partner?

....

....

....

Executive summary

When infatuation happens in your life. Say yes! See the gift that that relationship and that encounter brings. Melt with it, let there be air between you. Take care of your feelings, your feelings are your responsibility. Your partner is responsible for theirs. If it ends, life has something more to give you, something of higher value for your individual development. It is not the end. It is then something else life wants you to have and need. Cry out if you need to and increase your trust in yourself and life. In my case, I can only see when I look back on my life that every step and every relationship has gotten better. I have grown and fallen more and more in love with myself and life. Every relationship is a gift.

A love relationship can be seen as a zipper between the male and female within you that is mirrored outside in your partner. You, you are whole and help each other to be in that process. Higher and higher aspects of love. Communicate and dust off in the relationship all the time. Don't let it stop and dust again. Let your love be alive. You are both equally important.

Challenge

Let love breathe between you.

Dare to love, dare to give. Everything that happens in love teaches us to live. It helps us to grow. It may not turn out as you planned. But it will be as it should. Because we always get what we need. Dare to be yourself and listen to your inner self, and not lose yourself in the other.

Love is a natural inner quality, you can share it with your partner. Be generous, be true. The gift is from you to you and your partner is the opportunity to grow and expand in love. You need to learn to act and be adults. To learn to be able to communicate as adults about the family as a whole.

We believe that love is a pink shimmer where we should dance on little rose petals. Love is between two individuals. And it must be tended like a garden. A shared mission.

If we don't learn to grow with love, learn to express ourselves, listen, respect our partner and ourselves, the energy stops and no one feels good. When we get married or decide to live together, it is the beginning, not the end of the relationship. From there, find a platform for the connection and respect to grow. What do you want to give to your partner? What does he or she mean to you?

Can you forgive and let go? Can you say yes to her or him in your heart? Questions to keep alive within you.

Listen to your partner and take in. Let your partner listen and take you in! In your hearts you are one and that is where you meet. Keep that door open!

When two people feel attraction, the next aspect of the wheel of life can become a reality. Let it happen as lovingly as you and you can without forgetting about your relationship.

7. NOW FAMILY, YOUR FAMILY WHERE YOU ARE AN ADULT AND HAVE CHILDREN WITH A PARTNER.

*T*he opportunity two people have. To create a family.

One of the most important and one of the most difficult roles, to be a present, aware adult. Your children are the children of life and have their own longing and journey here on earth. Becoming with children can be easy. But acting as an adult parent and caring for one or more children is an incredibly loving challenge.

General

Being a good parent is probably one of the most important roles we have. To allow children to grow up and find confidence and power in themselves. However, we have never received any training in this.

The more aware you are of your history, your own childhood and the feelings you have from that time, the more present and supportive you can be for your children. Then you can act as an adult parent. Then your children can feel seen and feel good.

That is the gift to them. But unfortunately, we're just going through the motions and we often haven't stopped to take care of our own baggage. Because we are energy, children do not do what we say or think. They do what we do. They inherit the energy that we have. Just as we have done with our parents. Some things we have inherited for generations. And if we don't see that, we can go on for another few hundred years. Children are emotions, and if we can't relate to our own, how can we relate to theirs?

Share your love, take your role as an adult. And remember how it was for you as a child. Let your children be the children of life who have their own inner intelligence to follow.

About me

I chose not to have children. When my husband, whom I married at the age of twenty-three, talked about having children, I was shocked at first. I hadn't even thought about it. Then I had an intuitive feeling that I couldn't do it. My inner child needed me more than anything else. I knew somewhere inside me that if I have a child, I will have great difficulty bonding it to me. My inner pain and complicated relationship with my mother, the constant loss of not having had a mother who was there. A mother who for reasons I never knew or understood. I interpreted her rejection of me as meaning that it was impossible to love me even if you tried. I had no idea that she carried a deep, deep pain of not being chosen. For three years, she had been in an orphanage without coming to a family. When I first received this piece of the puzzle as an adult, all the pieces fell into place. As a child, I experienced pain and exclusion. I had never been particularly fond of playing with dolls or with small children. I forgot and hid my dolls in the closet in the countryside. I related to them as I felt my parents did to me. Forgetting that I existed and that I had needs.

Anyway, there were no children on the outside for me, which has meant that I put all my love on my inner self and then on all the clients' and course participants' little inner children. I have also always known somewhere in my mind that I have had a different path than the one with family and children in this life. Today I have children in my family that I love dearly. A little girl and her father whom I have taken under my wing. I am extremely grateful for this gift. That life has given me the opportunity to feel the unconditional love that can exist between a child and an adult. To love and be with the innocent energy of a child. Today I can also understand my mother better. Being a parent is one of the most difficult meditations in life. At the time my mother was not happy with herself and her life. She was an unwanted child and had carried that pain all her life. How could she take me in. If she had worked through her pain, grief and history, she could have loved me, her only little daughter. But now that wasn't the case, I had to do that job. The end of that suffering.

I love her today and her little inner child. The more understanding I have the more love I feel. There is nothing to judge, only understanding from a larger perspective. Then comes the unconditional love. Nothing else exists.

Client example

I don't often work with the children of clients who come here, because it's never the children's fault if there are problems at home. The problems always lie with the parents and the history they carry. The energy is invisibly passed on. I am determined to always focus on the mother and father, if possible. However, sometimes the children need their own support, someone who listens to their feelings and thoughts, without wanting to change them. A person who sees them. For example, when parents go through a divorce, children are victims under the circumstances. They have to accept the way things are. After a few years, when the situation has calmed down and everything has been resolved, the children's feelings may surface. This usually happens when things have settled down and they see that everything is working. That all new homes and possible new partners with their children and new routines are in place. Then they can dare to relax, which means that their feelings come to the surface. It can be difficult for parents to understand their children when they think "now that everything is so good!". Well, for them it is.

One client and girl who touched me a lot is Marie, who was ten years old when we met. She lived with her family, mom, dad, a sister and brother. I didn't know her parents but they had heard of me. The mother had done courses at BaraVara after my time there. The father had some resistance and did not want to start looking at himself or understand that the obsessive thoughts his daughter now had, had something to do with him.

He couldn't or wouldn't understand that Marie's strong obsessive thoughts were a reflection of the family's immense fear of emotions. The mother then came and continued her inner work with me. The father did some of my courses in a process that I then had.

Marie's obsessive thoughts meant that she couldn't watch TV, talk or even answer the phone. She could not use or look at a computer. The family had slowly started to realize that something was serious as she was no longer acting like the girl they had previously seen her to be. She was spending more time at home and not with her friends, she didn't answer the phone when it rang. She had become stranger and stranger in her behaviors. There were problems at school. When they went to watch a movie at school, she made up that she had a headache and went home. She was getting further and further away from her friends. She said she would call but didn't. Her control and obsessions got worse and worse. She and I started seeing each other. We saw the whole family. We all saw each other, her mom and dad. Her siblings, brother and sister. We met, just the children. We met, mom daughter, dad daughter. The mom and the dad. All to find the true and real roles in the family. On both the mother's and father's side, there were events and abuse that had caused both parents to shut down their emotional lives.

Marie and I built trust in each other. We worked on and focused on her awareness and love for herself. We saw each other every two weeks. We talked about our inner energy and about being human and being able to feel our feelings. We practiced in every way we could to increase understanding and rest in Marie's inner self. In this beautiful girl, she and I found a big dose of spiritual longing. And what she wanted to do most was to meditate together and get some healing touch. She loved when we were still and in touch with each other. All the time focusing on what was happening inside her in the world of thoughts and feelings. I felt a strong love for her and she fought on.

We set goals and what she wanted to achieve with her work and with herself. She was able to make a plan. A step by step plan. One of the points on this plan was to be able to watch television. For one minute. This practice would then be slowly increased. The first time she would watch, she wanted it to be with me. For one minute. We sat down on the couch, she cried and all the feelings and thoughts that she had had a thousand times before, we had written down on a piece of paper so she could see that it was old repeated patterns that were active. Not something new and nothing that was dangerous here and now. All these thoughts and feelings that she had written down on the paper were the ones that were constantly spinning and they controlled her whole life. Now she wanted to start challenging them herself to see who she was in all this. What was reality? She sat safely in my arms I was there with her and held the energy. It was one of the longest minutes of my life. But she made it!!! She cried uncontrollably first out of fear. Then in anger and finally in gratitude and joy.

After this round, the turnaround happened. She had taken her life in her hands, was no longer a victim of mind control. She could be present with her own feelings. Which turned out not to be dangerous. She could stay in the middle and she could rest in her heart that so beautifully began to open. She started practicing at home and her family supported her. We made a plan together. The family was really there for her. It was so wonderful to meet her, and our meetings became more and more loving and easy. We set clear structures and goals together. Making space for her feelings was one of them.

We met in September. We started up with the whole family and had our meetings she and I. At Easter they went to the Alps, something the whole family had loved to do when the children were young. But since the daughter couldn't use all the computers, it had been impossible for the last few years. This trip was the biggest trial by fire because all the TV screens and monitors that are everywhere in an airport. It was tough for her and I know that the whole family had to struggle to have a nice vacation. But it worked out. We continued in the spring with our meetings. During the summer it got easier and easier. In September, a year after we started, we were done with each other. That Christmas she wanted a computer for Christmas and she used her cell phone. She was then as was any teenager.

One year may sound like a lot. Or that it was not difficult to manage. But it is when control is so strong and the family had repressed many emotional memories. Before she met me, she had been offered to take tablets to cope with her situation. Something that neither she nor her parents wanted. This path of awareness and love went fantastically well. And I am glad that she chose it herself. She became free of her obsessive thoughts. Partly because she wanted to, partly because she was open to receiving support, and partly because it was a tremendous help that the whole family wanted to play their part. We had a good relationship. The mother and father did everything they could to take care of her feelings and her story. A sister and brother who were there to support. The whole family had to see and take responsibility for their parts. This was probably most difficult for the mother, who had always had emotional control and did not want to see what her childhood had done to her. Now the pieces started to fall into place and everyone in the family had to take care of their own feelings.

I love this family immensely for their courage to see and open up to all that was there. The girl's control over her thoughts had to do with many layers of repressed emotions. Her obsessive thoughts became a gift and an awakening for the whole family.

Becoming aware of your role as an adult, what energy and emotions we bring with us when we start a family. The children know you. You cannot fool them no matter what you say. They become carriers of the emotions you have not addressed.

Exercise

Do you trust in the inner wisdom and power of your children?

....

....

....

What do you bring with you that you see reflected in your family?

....

....

....

Do you and your partner have clear roles as parents together?

....

....

....

How do you deal with children's feelings? How do you relate to yours?

....

....

....

Executive summary

See clearly the roles you have in the family. Trust that children have their own inner wisdom.

Make a distinction between who children are and what they do. You are an adult and set limits. Provide opportunities for expansion. If there is a problem, the problem lies in the adult world and not in the child.

Take responsibility and see your feelings and how they are expressed. You are responsible for your story so that the children can create theirs. Process it so the children do not become carriers. If you can't be true to them and let them understand what your baggage is without feeling too sorry for yourself, take responsibility and reconcile with your own baggage. Let your children find their way. They are the future and they have their unique path. Listen and learn from them instead of telling them what you want and think. Life and wholeness are bigger than your thoughts.

The challenge

Being an adult.

Being aware of what are the feelings of your own inner child.

Living both lovingly and consciously. Clarity in the role you have. Being true to yourself.

Using words that nourish children and having harmonious views on how things should be. "I'm sorry that you perceive me or the situation that way. I love you with all my heart. And forgive me for not being able to do better than this right now. Thank you for being you and being in my life."

Being seen and connected is the most important thing!

Trusting that your child has all the knowledge they need within them. Self-esteem comes from learning to listen and follow our inner self.

Let your current family be embraced by an even bigger family. The next aspect in the wheel of life is about it.

8. FRIENDS, SOCIETY AND THE WORLD. YOUR TRIBE...

*B*eing in a greater we. Outer reflections of yourself.
Being able to step out of your own identity and just be yourself with friends.

In the society and world where we have our place.

Respect for their friends and the world around them.
Being able to take responsibility for your part in the bigger picture.
To be able to step into a larger context and find community.
Share their loving energy with the whole world.

General

We play important roles in each other's lives. Being able to play yourself with friends in a larger context where you can be yourself. Going from being a self to becoming one in a larger context. Friends who remind you and can support and give feedback in a constructive way.

Being able to love yourself, to dare to open up to a partner. Dare to live and expand in a job situation. Being able to be a parent. Reconciling with your history and then seeing your friends as a natural part of your life. To be able to live in balance and wholeness. Now, that's not always the case. Friends can be a wonderful support in achieving that balance. Friends can mirror ourselves where we are right now. So, depending on your own development and expansion, your friends may not always have been able to keep up. But if that's been the case, new friends tend to come into the picture. Friends are also the doorway to the larger swarm of friends that is society. What we live in society and the world in the outer circle. How do we live with it?

To be able to relax and melt with a group that you trust and can expand in. But also to be able to see that we are part of a larger context like our society and the world. Can we contribute our energy in an expansive and loving way?

About me

When I was identified with my pain, I often felt that there was no place for me.

It was difficult to be included among friends and society was something 'others' were involved in.

After my awakening and turning point, I felt that I was part of the whole universe and we were all one big family. What the future would hold, I had no idea. But it was like I needed to walk around and just be aware of everything that was around me. I had been home in Stockholm for a few summer months and every day I walked around and in gratitude silently said goodbye to everything that was here. The city with its wonderful archipelago and water. Where I got strength from nature as a child. Now it had been like a single kind of grateful goodbye that took place. This was nothing I thought, it just happened.

One day it was like everything was done and it just happened, and I went to bed with an open and grateful heart. I had gotten everything I ever wanted, I had come home. "Now God, I am ready to die. I don't know what to do here on earth anymore." I felt whole and had no desire for more. I lay for a long time in a deep harmonious relaxed state. After a while, I don't know how long, the needs of the body began to make themselves felt. An understanding came that it is not me but life that will "use me". I was not going to die or leave this life and this day at all.

But just before my eyes opened, a question came from deep within." Is there anything you long for?" The answer came quickly and naturally. "I would like to have conscious and happy friends, people around wherever I go. When I buy food, fill up the car, at the bank etc." My answer, as I see it, was that I wanted to live in a more conscious and loving world. That was what my life was going to be about. At that moment I understood it. Not how it would happen, just that it was the desire that lived in me. I never needed to plan or know. Life and longing did that.

Today I can fill up my car, buy food, travel around the world and meet people who have increased their awareness and live more loving lives. The longing knew and I know today that many thousands have today awakened through the longing I then became aware of.

I had no choice to help or contribute to society and the world. But life did. Desire had it. Something that, looking back, I am extremely grateful and happy about.

We are all here together and we all have our unique role to play. It either has an expansive and constructive impact or we hinder each other from growing and thriving.

Client example

Friends are rarely a problem or a topic that clients or trainees tend to bring up.

But I remember a young guy who came with a problem that bothered him a lot.

Peter, a thirty-year-old engineer. He had a problem with his hands sweating so often. He had seen it as a nervousness when taking on new challenges. He was really suffering from the problem. It was obvious that his body was having a reaction. We started as I usually do with the current situation. He had a girlfriend but was not living together. He was not ready for that step yet. He had a new job since two years. A job he liked. His first real one after graduation. He loved cycling, skiing and sports. He was a vibrant young man. But his hands were causing him a lot of problems.

He had a lot of guy friends who used to meet up and have a beer. But his problems made him avoid seeing them more and more.

We looked at his story. A mother and father who were still there for him. He was the second child, two years younger than his older sister. Peter and his family grew up in a small Swedish town. Everything had been calm according to Peter. We continued to investigate what could be the cause of his hand sweat. He told us that his grandmother and grandfather had been close to the family and lived in the same town as them. When Peter was 11 years old, he had moved to a different school on the other side of town and made new friends. He had found it a bit difficult at first to get into the class. But it had gotten better and better. Peter didn't remember exactly when it happened, but during his first semester at the new school, his grandfather died. Which caught his mother's attention. He himself was sad about what had happened. As he was already a bit fragile from the new school situation, he didn't want to take more attention. He didn't want to be another problem for his mother. He kept his feelings, his fears and his sadness inside himself.

One day in the schoolyard, a fight breaks out and he gets caught in the middle. He is teased and he fights to defend himself. In the middle of the fight, two teachers come and stop the fight and Peter is taken aside. He is filled with emotions that stop there and then. His fear of what will happen at the principal's office is one of them, another is how he will be able to cope with his friends and his situation at school, but mostly he feels fear of how his mother will cope with him and this situation. He thinks he's going to wet himself, which he doesn't. But after that day his hands started sweating. He cried and he cried when he realized how deeply this was embedded in his body.

That's what emotions do, they settle in the body. Now, finally, he could understand and connect the event with the reaction of his hands. It would have been too painful to deal with it then. Instead, he had defended himself by saying that it was natural because he played soccer, ran, jumped and was lively as a boy is in his teens.

Now in our inner work, he was able to embrace and understand the guy he was then. He began a reconciliation work with himself. But also the reconciliation work he needed to do with all the guys he had fought with and against during his school years. Some of them had become close friends in the later years at school. But in the subconscious, the memories remained. The hands helped him to get in touch with those emotional memories so that he could heal himself. That's how the mind works. The body, the emotions and our inner nature are one and the same.

By seeing and understanding so that all the pieces come together, healing happens. Just like for Peter.

The expression on his hands slowly faded. But above all, he could relax and not hold himself back. He was no longer angry and separated from what was happening. His hands became his friends. That helped him to understand himself. He could tell his mother about what had happened. She hadn't suspected anything at the time, she had been preoccupied with her own father's death.

Their love and respect for each other's journeys deepened.

Now Peter was able to go out with his friends again in a new relaxed way. He dared to get closer to his girlfriend. He had come closer to himself and become his own best friend.

Exercise

What kind of friends do you surround yourself with?

....

....

....

What is it that you want to share with other people? What does it mean to share the best of you when there is contact?

....

....

....

What is your approach to society and the world? What is your contribution in this world? Do you give what you want?

....

....

....

What would you like it to look like if it were optimal ?

....

....

....

Executive summary

Friends are an important part of your life. Allowing the group of friends to be alive.

Friends give you a reflection and a sense of reality about where you are.

We are all one and we all come from the same source. We all have everything within us. We are all love even if in pain and events we have had to shut down. We all have feelings, we all have a story that we carry. The more I reconcile with mine, the more I can love and understand my friends.

Challenge

To see your role in a wider context. Friends, society and the world.

When all the roles we have are allowed to live and be filled with our love, presence and potential, it is extremely valuable to stop. To be able to step out of our doings and identifications and just be. To allow stillness, silence to fill our lives. To step out of the way of ourselves. Become one with the whole. Allow the next aspect to take you home in yourself in depth.

Your inner SOURCE, BUDDHA NATURE AND WHOLENESS.

This aspect of the wheel of life is the most important. It is the origin of our whole life. It is where we come from and it is where we will one day return to. It is the base, it is who we truly are. Every cell knows, you are pure divine universal energy. Beyond all concepts and ideas of who you are supposed to be is the true this living source of pure divinity. That which witnesses and just is. Allowing this quality to permeate all areas of your life. You come from this source and are not for a moment separated from it. You are life, you are natural love. You are divine without values or thoughts of what 'God is'. It is here within you that you can find rest and power beyond the confusion and doing of the mind. This is where our inner awareness and buddha nature can come to life. In our time of so much doing, it is extremely valuable to stop and give space to just be. To find an inner space where we can rest beyond the noise of thoughts and constant traffic. Here is our source and here we can replenish our batteries. This energy embraces and is in everything. To live from here is to live in total harmony with what is. Everything is allowed to be as it is. Without awareness of this aspect, we lose perspective in our lives. With awareness, we can allow this source of wisdom and inner contact in everything we do to be present in our lives. An inner contact that is constantly there. It is not personal but one with the whole and the entire universe. We all have and are this divinity. This contact with ourselves provides security and self-confidence. It is from this place within us that we can witness and see what is happening in our lives. A witnessing and seeing without judgment. A being in harmony with what is.

We all come from the whole. We are all the whole. It is the space that embraces everything. The space that is in everything. Inclusive and non-judgmental. Beyond the idea that there is any separation between us as individuals and the whole, life or divinity. To be able to see and understand that this quality is always with us in life.

Everything that happens in the outer world is impermanent. To find one's inner nature, one's inner heaven where everything comes and goes.

Your inner self is divine. Let it expand and permeate your life. It already does, but with the awareness of it comes relaxation. Allow yourself to come home and rest within yourself, to be able to be empty of history, thoughts and ideas about the future here and now. Find your connection with divinity. In nature or within yourself. Beyond all concepts and learned ideas. Your impersonal, timeless knowing and witnessing, is this invisible force behind and beyond all identification. This emptiness that we can call witnessing to life. The beyond form and identification. Open and completely empty. An emptiness where life can come again.

This quality that has always existed and will always exist. There is total harmony and balance.

Learn to rest in and listen to the inner silence. Ask yourself the question. Who is it that thinks, feels and experiences? Who experiences the body and all sensory impressions?

When we can allow this quality to expand and gain more and more space, it creates a greater resonance between you and the whole.

This resonance and stillness is filled with life potential that was our true nature. This filled emptiness that exists in every cell. When our mom and dad had their love meeting and the wonder of us coming into being and being formed has its origin in this potential. What we come from before the form appeared. Learning to rest and come back to this quality helps us not to get stuck in different identities on the outside. Identities that change over the course of life. Every cell, every breath has its origin from this divine source. It is you...

An enlightened person lives from this place. A so-called enlightened person is not identified with the form. That which comes and goes. A fully enlightened person is just this emptiness with the body as a 'shell'.

That place that is in harmony with the whole universe and the whole. The place where no separation or ego structure stands in the way. The presence that is without any personal identification. The place within us that just is. The place that sees without choosing or judging. It is free from all tables or musts. When expressed, it is unconditionally loving, it is everything. It is a silent, still presence with a silent witness. We as individuals all have this place within us. We can begin to know ourselves beyond all concepts, ideas, thoughts and our history. To step out of the events and activities of life and just allow ourselves to be in stillness for a while. The more we allow ourselves to do so, this place within us expands and we gain greater confidence in life. Realizing that the self is the wisdom, is the emptiness and the everything. Unconditional love. For me, the taste of that quality is extremely important. My history sometimes reminds me and I fall into old patterns. Then I need to take a turn with the illusion of myself to relive the still presence I am.

Our egos and personalities that constantly want our and others' attention are slowly being replaced by a loving presence where the wisdom of life, of the present and of silence is given more space. The pure, empty innocent energy we truly are. The one that has always been, and always will be.

Find the doorway to the stillness, peace, harmony and the whole universe within yourself. Learn to rest, come home in this place within you. When we live from here, there is no end station, only eternity.

Learning to be nothing. Beyond the ego's ideas of who we think we are. To be able to 'just be', living our unique energy from a place of trust and openness. Without holding on. To let ourselves be lived.

When we no longer let a fear of what is to come control us or that life is something that does not wish us well. When we learn to live in trust. Grounded in the present and totally open to the fact that life will take us wherever we want to go. When we can live in harmony with the whole universe without being separated. Then there is no beginning and no end. Just a witness to all the forms that transform and change. Forms come and go while awareness is constantly present with its witness.

You are the one who vigilantly sees.

Our inner source and buddha nature is within us all. The part that is beyond the story of who we think we are. It is there but is often completely suppressed. When it is allowed to come to life, it can expand and our being can then lovingly be present in all parts of life.

It is the core within us that remembers the universal order. The universal wisdom.

Here and now. And nowhere else.

When we are, we live and act in harmony with what is.

"Sitting silently,
doing nothing,
the spring comes
and the grass
grows by itself"

LAO TZO

General

Wisdom is found in presence, in awareness beyond thoughts and history. We all have a history that makes itself felt in the different contexts of life. We have roles that we need to live and take responsibility for. We need to live and make money. But our lives can be transparent. We can allow ourselves to step into ourselves and draw strength and wisdom from the silence and harmony within. We can act and live and then come home within ourselves and rest in the emptiness. We can use yoga, which is meditation that brings the body and mind together. We can use different meditation techniques. We can dance, we can paint. We can find different 'bridges' to take us home into our BUDDHA nature. Whatever technique we use, the focus is on stepping out of our personality and identification to just be "nothing", to be able to merge with the whole. Our inner silence and divine emptiness is in tune with the whole universe. Like the wave that is one with the sea, we too are one with the whole. Allowing ourselves to remember and come home to the whole gives us strength and clarity.

This wisdom is an incredible gift to rest in.

About me

When my mother died, it wasn't death I was afraid of. The fear was of facing my own feelings that I was already carrying and had stuffed down. The question that came was more existential. What is the meaning of life? That this, my little life, with all its events and pain cannot be the meaning. That there must be a bigger picture, something I could not see. Through my life journey that I told about in this book, the turn came when I could see that the story of me was not who I am. The filled lovingly vibrating emptiness is me. Awareness, that is who I am. nothing else. beyond the feelings and thoughts lay the truth. That fullness, emptiness that is one with everything. This vibrating infinite presence. It is me, it is who we are. The wave on the sea. The drop that contains everything. Life forms that come and go. We are not this form, we are what sees. The sky that embraces the clouds. The clouds that are one with the sky. Or in my case the energy had frozen, but with awareness and loving presence with my inner self I began to melt and become one. Without awareness of who I am, or we are, that wholeness, freedom and unconditional love is everything. In the center of it all I found this source and buddha nature in me that was true and pure and in touch with everything.

In this energy there is only peace. It has been here that I have found my trust, my peace and all the nourishment for life. It has been here that I have been able to rest and find energy in my life. Here I have experienced myself whole in harmony.

This presence was and is what I see as the most important thing to become aware of. This presence beyond our identification. Here there is, as the Buddha once said, a witnessing.

When I started my inner journey and met myself, it was this realization that made my whole life transform by itself. The question of who am I if I am not my story? That question was answered by this infinite quiet silent present loving embrace. Who we are before we are born and where we go back to when the identification with this life is not in the external. As children, this quality had been so natural. This contact with that which is greater than me.

So in the beginning, therapy was necessary. To become aware of how it had been and what it had done to me. After an awakening, the work begins to constantly dust off the illusion about yourself.

But the most important part was to experience who I was beyond history. There I was free, everything was as it should be. Nothing was ruined. Wholeness was everything. Like a sky behind the clouds. then is not harm even if lots of clouds have hidden it. The presence of now, nothing else exists. A witnessing and seeing without any thoughts coming in and thinking. Everything is harmonious and empire balance, living and vibrating unconditional love. The me that I thought I was, existed but it was no longer me.

This now is a perishable commodity and therefore it is a living quality to remember and stay in. When thoughts come in and blind you. See them, examine them. Are they true for me right now?

Again and again. To go from the outer shell of thoughts. Feeling the feeling. Embrace in an acceptance. Experience the love as it happens. Asking who am I? To then land in a stillness. A being. Without identification. To just "drop" into the here and now in the void and the center we all have and truly are.

The years with Osho allowed me to expand in this quality. Meditation techniques that helped me again and again to land in the present. Not only to get the enlightened help to find home. But also together with others to live and be in a new way. A conscious and loving way. To see that it is possible to live in a completely different way. As an organism where each part does what it should in harmony with the whole.

The meditations I was lucky enough to come into contact with were modern and transformative.

Osho, a mystic of our time created them for modern man.

They were and are absolutely amazing. They transformed my whole being again and again. For many years I had them as my only pillars to rest in my mind. Unless I was in India, where I devoted all my time to meditation. To constantly dust off the inner mirror so that the mind can be empty and pure. To let the heart with its wisdom be open and alive.

The morning meditation looks like this.

Dynamics: With different five parts.

Powerful irregular breathing. Focusing on the exhalation. Breathe only through the nose.

Then living out the energy, emotion, sadness, anger, fear, joy in motion. To open the stubborn and bring to life.

Then jump and bump the energy from the base and up with a mantra "ho" which was originally a "who am I".

Then full stop with a totally "frozen" body to witness more clearly what is happening.

Then dance where the body itself guides you, you just follow along. A living energy that then follows us into the day.

The afternoon meditation which is one of my favorites. It has been able to transform me so wonderfully many times in life.

Kundalini: With four different parts

It takes us from the energy of the day and home into rest.

It starts by allowing the body to shake freely. Shake loose and free itself.

Then dance. The way you feel your body and energy want and need.

Then to stillness, standing or sitting.

Then more stillness and a non-being with lying down on your back and just letting yourself relax completely.

Both of these meditations, and many more, are available in personal development bookstores and online.

There are lots of techniques that have the purpose of bringing us home into our inner center and BUDDHA nature.

Meditation or mindfulness. It is important to find the paths that suit us so we can give ourselves over. It is valuable if you can do it with others as the quiet silent inner nature can be experienced so much stronger if you are more. The silence deepens and can sometimes almost feel like you can touch it. That was one of the gifts of being in India with Osho. We were several thousand individuals either working, meditating or doing group processes. All in a form to increase their presence. Then we all gathered at the morning and evening meditations. And the most powerful and beautiful thing for me was when we all sat in silence every morning and every evening to just take in the presence that was there when Osho sat with us. Either just silent or talking. The experience for me was that we were all one. Our identities disappeared.

Whether we were therapists, cleaning, chopping vegetables. Stood and welcomed people. Or making groups like a madman. We were all one in this silent divine presence.

In this silent living vibrating presence there is an intuitive wisdom. We miss this wisdom if we believe and live from the thoughts that build their intelligence on old information. On a completely different situation and time. The wisdom that is in the present is a wisdom that is in touch with the whole universe... With the wholeness of listening and allowing that wisdom to guide and live you is a gift. Step out of the way of the thinking mind, where all thoughts pass and this wisdom becomes your true self.

Our therapeutic journey continues until it is no longer activated in our lives. Knowing that I can embrace and rest in something greater and constantly come home within myself, here and now, this quality grows and our witnessing increases without losing ourselves in unconsciousness or our old patterns. We get a more enlightened life.

Let your energy flow. Let it be alive. To rest in your center and inner source and buddha nature is to be able to be alive. Spontaneous and have free energy flow.

Many misconceptions are there when we live from our thoughts and intellect. "So I'm just going to sit down and meditate for the rest of my life and do nothing more", no that's certainly not the case. Acknowledging and allowing yourself to live from within is a living journey. In my case, this journey has given me an adventure with a lot of work. Many events and experiences beyond what I thought possible.

I'm sure it's the same for you if you look. The source of life guides and sustains us. Not the other way around.

Client example

A client for many years. A man with a wife and a child. He is the youngest child of three siblings. His father was an aggressive man who constantly beat his mother. In order to survive her situation, as my client saw it, the mother had drunk alcohol. The man who had become co-dependent on the mother had also started drinking. He had struggled with his emotions throughout his childhood. His drinking was the only solution he had to cope with the family situation. The father's aggressions and outbursts had been many and for a long time. My client's siblings had started using drugs early on and disappeared more and more.

He was the youngest and sloppiest child, having managed to stay out of, more or less, the family's destructive behaviors and life. But he carried and bears the dysfunctional pain of the whole family.

When we met, he had hit the wall and was on sick leave for burnout. He had stopped drinking earlier in life but now it had come back and he felt incredibly bad. He really didn't want to but hadn't found any other way. We worked to deepen our understanding of his situation. We worked with his feelings and to put his inner family in order. But the path that came to his rescue and has worked for him is meditation and healing. He expressed that meditation was his only way to survive. There he feels he can let go and just land in the form of meditation and in the present. To go straight into the emptiness. With the healing, which I gave him, came the replenishment of pure new loving energy.

Working a lot with his emotions, even if it was hard, was possible when he had meditation and healing.

In the beginning we tried to sort out his history with his mother, father and the pain that had been there. He did as much as he could emotionally cope with.

Nowadays he lets it be as it was. He looks at it with more understanding and indeed with the love he could feel as a child.

He can see and he understands. That is enough. Through his conscious journey, all his needs to use alcohol have disappeared. Alcohol was used to numb emotional pain, among other things. He no longer needed it as he could allow himself to feel and not stuff them down anymore. His involvement with his mother disappeared when he realized that her pain went way back to when she was a child. She was not his responsibility. He could not save her either. He could only save himself. His processing had helped him and with new tools, meditation and healing, he had found an inner peace, love and a rest in something greater. If we are to break an addiction or pattern, we can only do so by replacing it with something of greater value. Otherwise we are just moving the addictions around. Higher value is love, understanding and rest. Finding those within. The place within each of us that is always there. That's what I helped him with. That is what all awareness does.

The way we meet today is that I send healing to him at a distance. This if he feels that he needs extra filling.

Here's how it can work: I sit down and allow myself to become as neutral and open as I can in the total presence of myself. I open up to the whole by tuning in to him. I have some rituals that help me with that. Then I let presence just expand out into wholeness with him. Ending with a ritual that I feel is valuable to me and him. The response that I get is always overwhelming. It seems that this way of empowering another human being beyond the tangle of thoughts . It is extremely valuable. He is blessed and so is his wife who sees the difference. He doesn't live in Stockholm so we book an appointment. Then we have an hour together in silence and conscious presence. His experiences become bright and loving. His inner self expands and he feels clarity, security and trust again.

I sit at home and just focus on his inner divine pure energy. However it works, he usually experiences that a deep relaxation occurs and he lands home and in himself. In the deep relaxation, as I see it, two things happen. One: we come home to our true nature where only love, harmony and peace prevail. Two: our subconscious then changes from being destructive to falling into its natural true flow. If we haven't worked with our history and emotions before, it can be helpful to consciously address them first. See more about that in the reconciliation exercise I write about later in the book.

Here are some of his comments today after:

"Pieces are starting to fall into place, I am crying with humility. Everything became very clear to me today.

Now everything is soft around and in me again. I really don't want to dust again. I'm starting to realize that I'm the one creating the main role in my life."

The insights he shares come from within himself. With strong support through the healing, silent presence, he can feel and hear the inner truth of who he is.

The healing takes his attention to the space that embraces everything. From thought, feeling and experience to the infinite space around us. The silence between the notes, the sky between the clouds.

Resting in oneself is not about being holy or finished.

It's about knowing that I am this quiet, vibrant, peaceful inner nature.

From the inside out. The destructive forces that previously unconsciously ruled his life are replaced by peace and loving experience and in the presence of himself.

For him, it is a vacation every time.

It is for him like dusting a mirror. Each healing session brings him a clarity. A feeling of being at home in himself where only peace and joy of life exist.

He can be present with his family. All worries disappear.

The more our identity falls into the still presence, the more the feeling of eternal life comes within us. The experience that the body is the shell and we are identified with the energy that is in the present. The awareness that sees and observes still and silent

You are the invisible buddha nature that has no form or time. The eternal emptiness that permeates everything. This awareness that sees, witnesses and is. Beyond all identification with the body or events. The more this presence is allowed to exist in your life, the more enlightened your life becomes.

Finding one's inner divinity and inner source is a human right in my opinion.

Healing happens when we can allow ourselves to be in that space. And me "giving" only reinforces that quality.

Exercise

Sit or lie down. Put on some quiet music. Let yourself rest and just relax. Turn off phones and external distractions if possible. Tell your family that you want to be left alone for a while. That you are going to have a meeting with yourself.

Let your thoughts be like birds in the sky. Let them fly free.

Let emotions and sensations be there without you "doing" anything with them.

Just let everything be. Let yourself be.

Let breathing be your pillar to cling to.

Watch the air come in. Follow it into your body. Let it take a moment to land in there. Then follow it as it leaves your body for a while. Let it take a second or so. And let the next breath come by itself. Just watch as if you were sitting in a movie theatre and just watching.

Nothing to do, just to rest in your inner peaceful presence. Nothing to think. Just being with yourself.
Who are you without being identified with your thoughts, feelings, sensations or actions?

....

....

....

What do you experience when you rest in your inner source and emptiness?

....

....

....

What would it be like to live from this emptiness and vibrating presence? Practice seeing and trusting that everything will happen as it should. That spring will come and the flowers will start to grow by themselves.

It is not only in the flowers that the energy knows. Even in you it is so, allow yourself to happen. Trust!

....

....

....

Who are you in this infinite universe? Where do you get your guidance and inspiration from?

....

....

....

Try for one day to let life happen without taking anything personally. You act and do what you are supposed to do. Letting everything happen without identifying yourself or taking credit. It's as if you're floating along and not caught up in what's happening. Letting the present guide you all the time. As if "you" did not exist.

Write down your experiences.

....

....

....

Life is constantly changing, energy is moving. If we look at the wheel of life, we see that we, as unique individuals, are born into an origin story that has been going on for a long time before we came to earth.

If we don't become aware of what it has done to us, we carry it around with us in all the different aspects of life. That life has its different aspects is like a diamond being cut. Different ages, different challenges. To flow with and do what we should in life. Allowing our inner self to expand and guide us more and more. To become who we already are. To be able to live closer and truer. To live in the natural flow. When life is allowed to happen quietly and calmly as it should. When we have stepped out of the way of the mind's constant chatter and blinding curtains. Then we can rest in the greater awareness and loving wisdom that is always available. In this source and filled emptiness, we come into contact with wholeness and the whole universe. As our identity shifts from outer form and doing to being, we gain confidence in what is our true nature beyond all form. Where we are one with all eternity and the universe.

We, the human race, have forgotten what is our natural source. We have surrendered our lives to thoughts and ideas that we did not even help create. To step out of the way, zoom out and start looking at our lives. Question and see how and what do I want with my life. What is true for me. Do I want to live the way I do or do I want to feel more love, joy, belonging and creativity, inside and out. If you want more of you than what is today, you have all the possibilities. Give yourself everything you need. You are the friend you have been waiting for. When your inner buddha nature is allowed to expand and get more space, a resonance is created. That resonance meets the whole universe. That resonance is completely devoid of ego, identification and personality. It just is... It is who we truly are....

ACTIVATE YOUR OWN WHEEL OF LIFE.

*L*et yourself feel, experience and be who you are. Wright paint and see what wants to come…

Your current situation.

What is your life like today? Draw a true NOW picture. It is important to start here and now. This is where the energy is. We can only change what we are aware of and can see. So be honest with yourself. It is about you and no one else. The journey is between you and you. You and life.

What do your thoughts look like in the different aspects of life?
What do you feel? Take time and feel it.
How do you live when you think and feel like that?

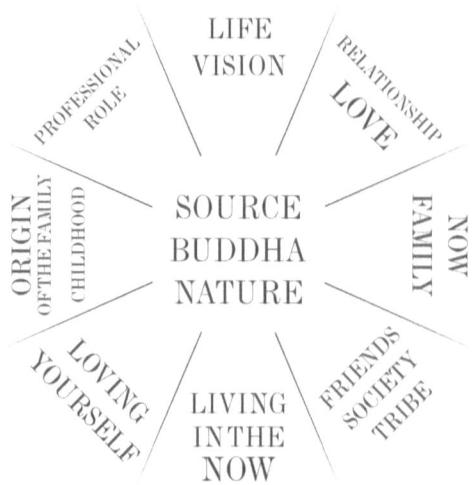

Empty wheel (center should be included)

YOUR LONGING AND VISION OF LIFE.

*W*hat would you like your life to be like?

What would it look like if you LIVE IN TOTAL HARMONY and harmony? What qualities do you see yourself living if they are in harmony and love? How would you live your life if you were free and without baggage?

Dare to listen to the longing that naturally exists in your heart. Dare to be true and clear. Let playfulness fill and open you to yourself. It's about living yourself in the truest way you can, to make yourself happy. Listen to your inner self.

What would your life look like if you had confidence in yourself and life and let the new take over? What do you need to do to realize your longing?

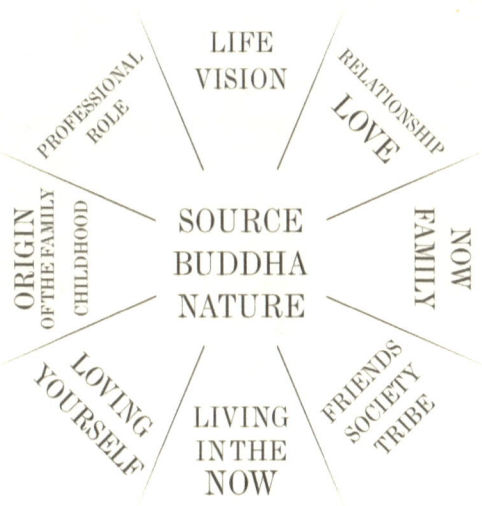

Empty wheel (center should be included)

WHAT CAN YOU DO OR NEED TO DO TO CHANGE YOUR LIFE SITUATION? WHAT IS HOLDING YOU BACK?

*W*hat do you need to create the life you want and desire? Any change in your outer life starts with changing your inner environment. Getting out of your own way and seeing your life without old thoughts, ideas and emotional memories. That you can create space to listen to your own voice and your own inner longing.

Do what you can, set milestones. Don't run away. Start walking. Say yes to yourself. Give it all you've got to create the life that lies within your potential. We are not special but each of us is unique. Only you can live this part of the wheel of life that is you. If you see and have a vision, dare to take one step at a time in that direction.

Do what you should and want to do.

If you have no vision, let yourself be open and receptive to what life wants. Remember life will come to you. Dare to write down your dreams and your longing, but also be totally true to what it looks like today.

Dare to affirm the life energy within you. How can your life be better than it is today?

Saying yes to expansion in love, success, harmony and truth

The art of saying YES! And dare to say yes to realising your harmonious future. To be able to be true and total. To see your life vision what it could look like. And then finding a structure for how we can step out of the way of ourselves so the flow of life can take us there . Maybe already now!

Be true to yourself. Truth is not a universal morality. Only you know it. When you put it into words, a change begins.

Your life, your freedom to live with yourself and the desire that lives in you to say yes!

Freedom to go with life. Freedom is never against anything. It is with you and your yes even your inner longing.

To start moving in the direction you long for and feel is true for you.

Your life, your opportunities. Make a plan, starting now. Write down a structure that can start now. Write simply and what feels possible. Give yourself space to become more and more alive, mobile, fluid in life. The energy is looking for the sea. Say yes and come along.

When you see how you feel now. Write it down clearly.

Then write down what you would like it to look like when there is harmony in your life.

Then you have choice and the opportunity to change and transform. It is a natural expansion.

Is there anything you see you can do to make a difference today? Or want to do.

Start moving in the direction you want. Start now. One step at a time. Trust your own legs, they carry.

Is it the case that you cannot influence, which is very rarely the case. Well, then there is only one way to approach it, to have the confidence that everything will happen perfectly. Change will happen when it should. Wait for you and life. Patience as when we have planted a seed. Everything happens when it should.

Life wants the best for you. Be open and receive.

Things may not always turn out the way we want. But it always happens as it should. And what happens, always happens with a higher value. We may not be able to see it in the moment. But with a little perspective, we can see.

Sometimes happiness and what you long for is just a thought away.

Be true to yourself. Dare to be true and see the present as it is. Accept and find the direction that you feel is true for you.

Clear away the thoughts that get in the way.

Know your longing. Trust that your longing and the longing of life are the same.

That longing is what life wants.

Feel that power and start taking steps in that direction.

Here and now, one step at a time.

It doesn't matter how fast we run if we run in the wrong direction.

It doesn't matter how slow it goes if it goes in the right direction. Then we can enjoy the journey.

Enjoying the journey of life with yourself. In harmony with the whole.

In my case

I found that I was not my history or my old emotional memories. It was like everything in my outer life just fell away. It was like I no longer needed what was there. The job ended, the relationship ended, it was like peeling an onion. Nothing I did, it happened. Total harmony, trust and happiness was my experience for a long time. It's like when we climb a ladder, with each step we take, we can see more and more clearly, the higher up we go. New levels of awareness awaited. There were other things that would come to me in life. I had no idea of all the gifts life would bring.

My vision of life is to be able to live openly, to say yes and to live and follow what is true for me in harmony with the whole. To live in trust, to say yes to life. It came a long time ago and is still with me. I have never had a lot of people around me, so for me, solitude has been an asset. It has also never been anything but total for me. I've said yes and taken on the challenges and given it my all. Not because I thought so, but because it just happened. With each step, the journey within me has deepened. If I had my own agenda, that agenda has always turned out to be wrong. What has come out has been far higher or bigger than what I in my "small" world could think of. To live in harmony and trust in what is the gift to myself and life.

My life became and is my meditation. Life became and is my love affair. In it there is harmony and happiness. We are one!

Make a plan for your dream life. And be open to life giving you everything you need.

Be open to the possibility that it will happen in ways you had not imagined. If it doesn't, life has a higher plan for you.

Exercise

How can you support yourself to live in harmony, happiness and love? What do you need to raise your awareness about and what do you need to address?

....

....

....

Trust and listening to your inner self. What might it look like to be in this process with yourself?

....

....

....

What does happiness in the different areas look like to you?

....

....

....

What is the worst thing that could happen if you started affirming yourself and becoming happy?

You're probably thinking right now "there's nothing wrong with that", but in our subconscious lie the hidden brakes that stop success and happiness.

....

....

....

Let your wheel of life be alive. Dare to live and follow your dreams and desires. Let yourself expand. Let your energy and passion guide you. Allow yourself to live true and natural. Allow yourself to be you and no one else. It is your life that matters. Don't wait for others to come and free you, or see what you long for. Only you know that.

Allow yourself to live in the moment, receive what life gives, experience and feel. See your vision and then make a plan that you can start with today. Small steps. If you can't make a plan, just practice being open and receiving whatever wants to happen. Nothing can go wrong. If you feel you've taken a step that doesn't feel right. Adjust and learn. Life wants to be good to you. Do you want it too?

Reconciliation and forgiveness meditation/exercise. A help to free yourself.

Reconcile with yourself, the rest will take care of itself. It has nothing to do with right or wrong, or any morality…. It is just to free your self through truth and love. Reconciliation is being able to accept and transform your life, to let go of old thought patterns. To allow oneself to go from being identified with sadness, pain, events and anger to being able to choose to give life energy to peace and love instead. To dare to let go of what I can no longer do anything about. That possibility lives within us, in our own heart, nowhere else. To reconcile means to go from wanting to be right to wanting to be true and free. This can happen when we no longer want to be controlled by the past. When we feel that we need, want, long to use our energy to live WITH ourselves and not against ourselves and life. When there is an understanding and longing that wants to liberate, be done with. It has nothing to do with anyone else. The only thing needed is your willingness to go from being right to being true. *Reconciliation* means that you are willing to let go of what you no longer want to rule your life. Peace lives within you, find it and reconcile with what is in your way. Now, it is not in the mind that reconciliation can happen. It can only happen through an acceptance that brings a sense of freedom and love which in turn means wholeness beyond separation. Which means that the event or person you are angry with or fighting against lives within you. Which is good because it is only within you that you can find peace and happiness.

To be able to step out of your own way and let go of what belongs to what has been part of your life and is behind you. What has been but no longer needs to control your life and your actions.

To be able to let go and give yourself the freedom and space to live more fully.

Reconciliation means that we have a willingness to let go.

Not to fight against what is. This can be about events, people, life itself and yourself.

Reconciliation is letting go of the sword and no longer fighting against what is and has been. To be able to put true words to the feelings we carry. Not rationalizing away the pain but feeling it and opening the heart. It's about freeing yourself, not about the other person, even if we use them as a projection to see what we are carrying. An example if we have been left by a partner (may have been long ago). The truth is that I then carry a sadness, anger, etc. To be able and dare to admit to yourself that I am sorry that you left me. The truth is also that I really loved you. The pain and struggle within me has made me close again to feel it.

The truth is also that I did not understand your needs, but only looked after my own. Please forgive me for that.

Sitting down with yourself and just tasting this practice can transform an awful lot within you. It is like going from being identified with pain, sadness and inner struggle to be right to experiencing yourself loving, peaceful and able to rest in the present beyond pain and separation. That work on yourself affects your whole life. If each of us starts to sort out and reconcile within ourselves, starts to live more lovingly without having an inner war, it is extremely valuable for the whole planet. It is the beginning of bringing peace on earth. Many people live like that today. But each one of us is important.

The biggest and perhaps most important is reconciliation with life and that one day it will end. To reconcile and accept that reality fully. Then, if not before, we need to let go of all ideas of control and that we are the ones who know and control. On the day we leave this life and body, there is only one thing and that is to totally let go. If we can do that consciously and in love, we give ourselves a great gift. Reconciling with the idea of death and the laws of life is a good start and can be very helpful.

Something we can experience in different types of meditation and other events where only the present moment prevails.

This exercise has helped me immensely. I don't know how it came to me, but it has worked for me in many different contexts for almost thirty years. I have needed to free myself and reconcile with the boyfriend but also against the laws of life. I had been struggling against the reality that my mother died. Tex How could life be so cruel to take my mother away from me without me having understood? That reconciliation with life itself is extremely important for our humility, among other things.

This exercise frees, humbles and unties thought pathways and bands of emotional energy. This is how I have used it for me over the years. There is a Hawaiian healing practice similar to this called ho'oponopono.

Reconciliation is about you, not about someone else.

What other people think or say about you is not about you, only about what they think about you.

Only you know who you are and what your truth is. Find your truths. And live them.

Do you try to control what others think and do or do you want to let them live their lives and you follow your own unique path?

Take care of what is yours. When you feel peace within you, you feel good. The energy can flow.

Write a letter of reconciliation to all those you feel you have hurt or have hurt you. To past events, but most of all forgive yourself.

Then we understand that what has happened and been has been so for some reason. Now it's over and the only place it continues to live in is in your mind. Let it go and you can start living yourself fully.

Reconciliation meditation

I am sorry:

....

I love, accept or am grateful to you:

....

Forgive myself for not knowing better:

....

Thank you very much! I bless you. I do not know your path here on earth. I can only find mine!

The exercise is first directed towards a person or event. Then you turn it back to yourself.

The exercise can be written or can be done so that you say the words out loud to yourself. Let it be like a meditation in the present. Let it take you to a deeper peaceful truth.

It is a tool for those who want to be free from the past. Forgiveness has nothing to do with morality. It has to do with being able to relate to and accept what has been. An exercise and gift from you and your own heart.

An exercise that makes you freer in yourself. When we let the truth rise to the surface, it releases us and we become freer and we can experience stillness and peace within.

Reconciliation means leaving behind. That the past should no longer rule life.

To reconcile is to restore the natural order of love.

Exercise example

- I am sorry:
  "I'm confused, angry, sad because I can't meet your needs."

- I love you:
  "I like you so much and I have enjoyed our relationship/friendship so much. I really love you." "I'm working on accepting you and what happened between us."

- I'm sorry:
  "I'm sorry I don't understand you or can't give you what you want."

- Thank you for being in my life! I am working on not controlling the situation but understanding that you have your way here on earth.

  It is the truth that this person or event is and has been a part of and a gift in your life. No matter what it looks or has looked like. When we struggle to see that, it's like we are saying life is wrong. It should not be like this.

- Namaste!
  I know that I carry the whole within me and I know that you do the same.

From my story

It is thanks to a relationship with a man that I can write about this reconciliation exercise. It helped me in depth in a situation that was both serious and painful.

It was 40 years ago. The man threatened and intimidated me, wanted to take my life.... But when I found my way home, I realized that he was driven by his pain. I had fit into his pattern. He had fit into my patterns. I had been afraid of passive anger and had always focused on controlling it. I got the mirror of my life. This relationship opened all the dams. When my patterns no longer matched his. When my so-called codependency had transformed into a love affair with myself and life instead, he went ballistic. He wanted to scare me into becoming my old 'kind' and 'dependent' self again.

He didn't understand what had happened but interpreted my calmness as if I had another man and love affair. He became so mad and did everything to scare me into loving him and being the way I had been before. He who had never hurt me before or shown such tendencies jumped on me and would strangle me. I was locked up, pushed in and out of cars in dangerous car rides.

I finally broke free and got out of the relationship. Which was the only true real thing.

But he was so angry that he stalked me and showed up everywhere.

It was dangerous to have power struggles with him. I knew I could only go with my heart.

I did this exercise mumbling for more or less six months.

It worked.

However, it took me a few more years before I realized to turn it home to myself as well.

Reconciling with myself and life has made me free and lovingly calm. There is no guilt or anger to put anywhere.

- I am so sorry that it has come to this between us. I'm so sorry that I couldn't communicate what was going on inside me.

- I love you. Not what you do. In my heart there is only love for who I know you are.

- I'm sorry for not understanding you. That I couldn't do better.

- Thank you for being in my life as an extremely important piece of the puzzle.

- I bless you and know that you have your way and I have mine here on earth.

I did this exercise for almost twenty-four hours a day. It was like a silent mantra I repeated inside me. It made me feel safe and the experience was that it untied all negative bonds. I learned to live from the heart, nothing else was possible. That was how the energy was set right.

The turning point and the healing within myself looked something like this. It came many years later when I did not have this awareness before. But when it came, it was extremely liberating.

- I am sorry Premleena for subjecting you to that treatment, for not being more aware. For not seeing. That I let it happen. For not seeing the signals.

- I love me Premleena. I like who you are so much. I love and care with all my heart for the divine being I/you are.

- I apologize for not understanding better.

- Thank you for still being in my life. I *bless* me and my life. I see that everything has a meaning in everything that happens if we only have the will.

- Namaste!

To relate to oneself in the same way as to others. I love and forgive you, I love and forgive me. Forgiving and respecting ourselves is the most important thing we have to do.

I am stepping out of your way. I am stepping out of the way for myself. I am stepping out of the way of life.

Everything is as it is. Perfect and I take responsibility for my parts. Sorting out, forgiving and accepting life as it has been. Without everything that has been in my life, I would never have woken up. So we are here to wake up, if we are given that grace. From being victims and ruled by the past. To wake up to the truth that embraces us. The reconciliation exercise is a help that unties the energy that was previously bound.

It can also be used in your everyday life. When you are talking to someone who wants something from you that you do not want.

In a relationship for example.....

- I'm sorry you feel that way.
- I like you a lot, I appreciate that we work so well together.
- Forgive me for not having understood what it is like for you.
- Thank you!

Simply, it means that we don't get caught up in each other's thoughts, feelings and energy. That we allow the other to be who they are. And yourself as well.

Client example

A client of mine has a mother who wants to be in charge of his life all the time, in charge of his wife and children. The only way he has found effective when talking to her is to talk like this. Then there is peace between them.

"I hear you mom. I'm sorry that you perceived the situation that way". "Or I'm sorry you feel that way about me."

"I like you mom, I love you. I so appreciate you caring and babysitting when we ask you to, watering the flowers when we are away, taking care of the mail, etc."

"I'm sorry mom for not understanding how you think. That I can't give you what you want or need right now. I want to be on my side and my wife's side. This is our life"

"Thank you mom for being in my/our life."
"I bless you!"
"Namaste!"

We can also write it down and make letters of reconciliation, which we then burn or tear up and throw into the sea. Whatever we feel is true for us. We can also do as I did. Use it as a mantra that I muttered quietly inside me.

Try it and see how it feels for you. Find your way. All I know is that it's a powerful and simple way of untying old feelings and thoughts that lie dormant and bind the energy within us.

A simpler but equally powerful option is to say nothing to yourself:

- I love you
- I forgive and let go of what happened
- I bless you. You have your way here on earth, I have mine.
Namaste!

You can use these sentences as a mantra silently to yourself, saying them again and again. Or you can write them down.

What events, people or situations do you have that you long to reconcile with?

....

....

....

A loving good luck. As you gain more peace, peace and space within you, you can create more peace and peace between you and others. Then we create more peace and peace between you and life and the earth with its nature that we live on and by. Everything is connected. Inner peace. Outer peace. It starts within you. You are important for a more loving inner and outer life to happen.

You are important for a more loving world and future to happen. Otherwise, the unprocessed rules from your subconscious.

Another option to transformation is beyond words. A meditation, Atisha's heart meditation that transforms pain into love and acceptance:

You then breathe in all the pain in your heart and breathe out love. Close your eyes and focus on breathing in all the pain you feel for a particular person or situation. Breathe into your heart and then breathe out love. Sit for as long as you feel you need to in order to achieve peace within.

Today I offer transformational processes, "New Life Vision", where you can go into yourself individually, or in groups so that a real transformation can take place, where a living and integrated life can take place fully. Trusting yourself and life from awareness and your inner truths. To live naturally as you were meant to live. Everything I offer goes under the collective name "Passion from within".

NAMASTE.

*I*t feels quite natural for me to end this book with Namaste.
Namaste meaning I salute the wholeness in you.

During my years in India, I learned to use the word and it is so beautiful.

I salute the whole and thank the divine in you.

I salute the love, the peace and the truth that you are.

In you lives the wholeness and the place that vibrates with the whole universe. Start exploring and dare to meet this wholeness. We all have all polarities within us. Everyone has everything. We can learn to turn on the lamp of awareness and see. Where it is dark, light the lamp of awareness. No darkness can remain dark if we light a lamp and dare to see. Stop, see and understand.

The gratitude I feel to share is that we are all whole and nothing is missing from us. That we can live this wholeness through ourselves. We, life and the divine are one. That each of us is unique and lives what we are meant to.

We have darkness and we have light. When the lamp of consciousness is lit, everything becomes illuminated and transparent.

I'm not filled with a bunch of answers, just filled with the experience that life loves us. Filled with an emptiness that is alive and all the wisdom I will ever need. Filled with love and gratitude.

Dare to live WITH you and life. With a big yes! in your divine heart.

Let yourself be illuminated by the light of awareness.

Let your future be bright. Find confidence in yourself and in life. Learn to listen to your inner self. To live lovingly. These are some of the things I wish you had taken away from this book.

I lived in a dysfunctional family at the beginning of my life. Feeling of separation. I faced myself and discovered that I was not my story but the presence beyond it. The silence and divine love energy we all are. My longing is that we can all come back to it and live in love with each other. Out of the divine order that is the universe.

One day we will leave this life. If we find how to live in trust, with ourselves and life, we will be able to make the end of this life journey in awareness. That is the ultimate reality and test we all share.

- The first and only step is to stop and listen to what is true for you.
- Sort out your history, learn to reconcile and your history will let go of you and the past.
- Learn to live consciously and in love. With yourself and life.
- Listen to your truths, live in harmony with them. Dare to follow your own heart.
- Learn to rest and relax in that inner stillness and let that wisdom fill and carry you.
- Life is here and now, nowhere else.
- You don't have to struggle to get there. Everything happens as it should. Just flow with it! You are pure life energy, it is in itself only divine love. It is in te a thought but it lives in every cell - live it....
- Stop searching, find that everything is already here. Stop, your inner self is waiting! Find your Life Vision!

My life vision is to live in harmony, consciously following my heart. That we can all do it together. Getting back to our inner intelligence and wisdom. That is what must happen. To end inner and outer war. To live in harmony and balance with ourselves, each other and life. In love with what is. Life is a gift, a mystery. Let us see that mystery and let us begin to live in harmony together. As we are meant to live.

Kissed by life

"You wake me up every morning with a silent kiss.
Every morning, like a loving sea, you embrace me.
The only thing that stands between us, between me and your divinity,
is the fluttering curtain that the mind creates
It is the only separation that exists". / Premleena

Sweet Freedom

"Between every Breath, The rising and The falling.
Is Your happiness and true freedom" /Premleena

I am not

"Not The body, not The mind.
It all takes care of it self.
The one that see, can that be me?
In that I am". / Premleena

The source

"The calling from within
Passion rises and falls
All from within
The source speaking". /Premleena

For all of you who wonder why my name is Premleena.

I got that name from Osho and it means "endless sky of love" in Sanskrit. A beautiful name and "remember" to live by.

All client examples in the book have been rewritten and all have fictitious names.

Executive summary

Live open and rooted in the present. See that where you are right now is perfect. Everything you need is here.

Grow up from your history, reconcile with it. Don't let it become a grain of sand in your eye that blinds you. You are not it. It has given you an opportunity to grow. See who you are beyond it.

Learn to live lovingly. Allow the intuitive wisdom of your heart to take over. Empower yourself to live and be who you are. It is the most natural thing there is. Listen and say yes to your own truths. Give yourself time to listen to your inner self. Dare to be alive. Life and you are one.

Let your wheel of life become a living wheel of life. Let the parts of your wheel of life come to loving life. Share your love and let you have your different roles in a harmonious, unique and loving way.

Find the stillness and silence within you. Learn to rest in your inner true nature. Draw your strength from there.

Find trust in the wisdom that lives here and now, the one that silently guides you. Allow that presence to expand.

Get out of your own way and learn to live in trust and harmony with the whole. Take charge of your life.

In awareness and love with an inner connection.

You are not your story. Become aware by seeing and reconciling. You are divine presence.

Many seek happiness but few find it. It is not HOW things are in your life that is the problem. It is how we relate to what is that is the point. That we are struggling and stuck in events with our emotions and thoughts. We need to understand and release the energy we are. Become aware that the story we carry is just a story. Not the truth of who you are. To open your inner doors to your life energy. To dare to listen to your heart and dare to live with confidence in yourself and life. The way is to meet ourselves in awareness and love. Our insides are reflected in our outer lives. If we long for success, we need to see what is standing in the way in terms of thoughts and old emotional memories and put it right. To find the truth that lies in self-worth. If we long for love, what stands in the way? Find the love for yourself and the love that reconciles with the past. If we long for a change, it comes when we meet ourselves on the inside. Then there is a change in the outside. Our exterior reflects the energy we carry within us. We are not our history. Reconcile with it. Being able to free yourself means that we face ourselves. Without that story, we cannot expand and grow. When we bring our story to the table, it gets energized and starts flowing again.

To be able to sort out within ourselves so we can move from chaos, war and disharmony to feeling the natural order that is love, balance and joy to ourselves and life. Finding balance and harmony brings us happiness. Life wants us well and is with us. Life is not against us. To begin to feel it and live it is a great gift. To dare to be alive and have confidence in you and your life.

The way is by becoming more aware and understanding who you are in your life. Or rather giving up the idea of who you are. More letting yourself happen and experiencing yourself more from within awareness and alertness in the present moment.

It starts with you and it ends with you. The deeper the contact, the freer you are. Let you be a channel for the life energy. Let it be alive.

When you begin to rest in your center, your innermost being, in your buddha nature, it is as if you are resting in the arms of the whole universe.

Being able to see your roles and "play" them as lovingly and consciously as you can. See the whole and dare to live you. Dare to listen to yourself.

The wisdom of life and your truth and longing are the same.

Therapy is like cleaning up an overgrown garden.

To start cleaning up so that we can have the life that feels true and more loving to us. To allow the invisible intelligent force to become visible through everything you do in your life.

Understanding the different roles that we have in life. When we see that it is a role. I accept it and I live it. But I don't let it control me and it doesn't take over me and my life.

To be able to rest, see and just be so that the seeds I planted in my garden can grow and bloom at their own pace. The seeds I planted can be seen as the direction, life vision and longing that lives in us.

That's where meditation comes in. Witnessing without judgment, just being and living in the moment in full trust that everything is happening as it should.

To be able to live WITH you. Being able to live WITH life. Living WITH your partner. Playing WITH your children.

It is living in meditation. With the flow. To live in wholeness. And in presence.

Life has its wisdom. Listen to it.

It is intuitive and lives in the present. We can call the place it lives in your heart.

I can clearly see that life is happening for us.

What we need is:

Total presence here and now. A clear non-judgmental mind, an open reconciling heart and a willingness to let our source and inner nature come alive and guide us.

It is the art of living. To be able to just be you. To step out of your own way and let life live you. Finding the passion for your life, from the inside out.

It doesn't matter who you are or where you are. Everyone is equally valuable. Every snowflake is unique and so are you. You just need to start seeing where you are. Sort out your inner self. Get out of your own way. Listen to yourself and life, dare to be true and find the direction you long for.

PREMLEENA RECOMMENDS

*O*sho's meditations. There is no better way to let the life energy come alive....

Osho's therapeutic meditation processes: No-mind, Mystic rose, Born again, Women Liberation.

OSHO meditation resort in Poona, India. Here I wish all people to travel to lift themselves out of all old habitual patterns. Dance, meditate and live the love we all are.

Byron Katie's technique: The Work. A fantastic and obvious technique if you want to see who you are beyond the thoughts. To easily find your own truths

Breathing therapy, to increase emotional connection

Yoga for the body.

Singing mantra songs. For me, my favorites are Deva Premal, Miten and Manose. A divine gift to oneself.

Literature:

- Osho
- Byron Katie
- Eckhart Tolle
- The Seagull by Bach
- Kahlil Gibran

Fact box:

Osho international meditation resort
Byron Katie

Books, retreats, trainings, and individual work
Info@premleena.se
Www.premleena.se/com

THE REVERSE SIDE

*W*hat do you want from life and what does life want from you? Dreams without an inner anchor remain just dreams. Let yourself stop and examine what your vision is for your life or how you want to live. New life vision means that only you can know your truths and unique life path. Only you can breathe in your unique life. When you turn your gaze home, you discover that you are already whole, at home and free. There is all the potential that wants to make you blossom. All the answers and everything you are looking for live in your heart. Stop and look inside yourself. There lives the friend you have longed for.

My message is:

- stop
- sort out what is not you
- live lovingly
- find confidence in yourself and life
- you are not going to be someone, you already are....

Find the passion inside you and live it. You are born perfect and unique, trust it. You are cared for and loved down to the last detail. Learn to live openly in the present. Everything is here. With this book and my wheel of life it is possible. You are the friend you have longed for. Let your inner wisdom and naturally loving nature come to life. It's not how your life began that is the point it's how you choose to live you now that is

Premleena Wettergran
Osho therapist, course leader and transforming group creator. With more than thirty five years and thousands of individuals' transformation as experience. With her own inner journey and awakening as a base and her wheel of life as a help, this book becomes a matter of course in every person's hand. It can transform your life.

www.ingramcontent.com/pod-product-compliance
Lightning Source LLC
Chambersburg PA
CBHW021621120626
46545CB00001B/342